Getting Around with Google Maps

A programmer's guide to the Google Maps API

John Sly

CONTENTS

Who's this book intended for?

In almost ten years, Google Maps has become a quickly recognizable element online. From getting directions, to seeing their maps embedded on company pages. They offer basic location services all the way up to traffic and weather features. They are highly customizable, and are hard to avoid online.

This book is intended for those looking to create new geographical visualizations and really take advantage of some of the mapping options available today. Over the years Google has been able to build one of the most widely used mapping services out there and offers a great API along with it. Aside from just dropping a marker on the map, you'll be able to start creating some exciting tools that focus around the user, allowing for a really interactive experience.

This book will focus on mapping, specific to the Google Maps API. Light knowledge of JavaScript will be necessary. As the book progresses, it will build on what was learned in the previous chapters.

John Sly

Introduction to Mapping

In 2005 Google Maps was officially announced. Providing directs, satellite image overlays, directions, street views, Google guides users over 12 billion miles per year. Currently in place in 1.18% of the top 10,000 sites already, google maps has become a recognizable and dominant tool in the web world.

What are some things you can and can't do with current mapping options? So far I've been able to do just about anything I've tried to do, though some options require some creativity, and some require a decent webhost. I've created maps of businesses; mapped out directions, heat maps, and much more. The limitations that have been hard stops for me have revolved around Google's own limits. Mapping out directions, converting an address to a mappable point on the map, Google will limit how many of those transactions you make in a single day. While the numbers are high, sometimes you may have a list of 8000+ addresses that may need to be mapped, and at a current limit of 2500 geocoding requests a day, you'll just have to grow comfortable with taking a couple of days unless you're looking to put up some money.

Through out this book we will start at a very basic level that doesn't require any familiarity with the Google maps API, and then steadily progress onto more advanced topics.

So where do we get started? Since this will be done with JavaScript you can work locally from your own computer. If you have a web host, then you can work from there as well. Later on in the book we'll cover more advanced topics that will require the use of server side hosting and access to a database. Any current browser should work.

The first thing you should do is begin familiarizing yourself with the Google Maps API and their documentation. Below is the page maintained by Google that includes all of the documentation you'll ever need. This is updated as new changes and features are rolled out.

https://developers.google.com/maps/documentation/javascript/reference

How to use this book

This book is written for developers at all levels and assumes some basic understanding is already there. This book will walk you through the maps API starting with very basic examples. As you get to be comfortable with the basics, it will start bringing everything together for more advanced examples.

All of the work in this book can be found online. To view complete and working examples for you to follow along with as you work your way through this book, please download the examples from the link below.

http://www.slyscripting.com/downloads/mapping.zip

Chapter 1:
Creating your first map

Mapping is a pretty straight-forward process. Google has set up an API that makes it easy to get something on a page without a lot of knowledge of their API, allowing people of any level of familiarity with their API to start playing around with it. From there you can start playing with more options and creating some higher functioning maps. Unfortunately, the only down side is that just spitting out "Hello World" in the map wouldn't be the most basic example, but we'll start with a very simple one, getting a map on a page.

Create a new html document. Once created, you'll have to link to the google maps API source code. Place the following code between your <HEAD> tags.

```
<script type="text/javascript"
src="https://maps.googleapis.com/maps/api/js?v=3.exp&se
nsor=false"></script>
```

Typically I would advise against including this since it's coming from an external source that is out of your control, but Google is among the top web giants, and this API has been around for a long period of time without any problems. The load time will be minimal, and you'll be able to take advantage of new updates and bug fixes without any extra effort on your part.

Place this code below into the <BODY> tags.

```
<script type="text/javascript">
function initialize() {
  var myOptions = {
    zoom: 12,
    center: new google.maps.LatLng(42.3514201241086, -
83.07237023559571),
    mapTypeId: google.maps.MapTypeId.ROADMAP
  }
  map = new
google.maps.Map(document.getElementById("map_canvas"),
myOptions);
}
</script>

<div id="map_canvas" style="width: 900px; height:
800px;"></div>

<script type="text/javascript">
  initialize();
</script>
```

You should end up with a wonderfully simple map with Detroit at the middle of it. Now I'll break down everything we did, starting with the initializing function.

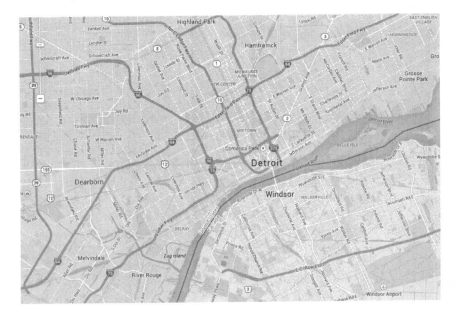

When we create a map, it requires some parameters to know what to load. It also allows for some optional ones. These can all be loaded from a set of options to pass along to our initializing map call. We set the center of the map, in this case, Detroit, Michigan. The zoom level, which gives the map, a decent focus on the city, where the lower the zoom level, the farther away we are. The last necessary parameter we'll set is the map type, which we'll set to a roadmap, the standard type you should be used to seeing. If we wanted to add any additional parameters, we could just add a line for any of them, such as, scrollwheel: false, which would disable the scroll wheel from zooming in on the map or noClear: false, to keep the original contents of the containing DIV for the map.

```
var myOptions = { … }
```

In the next line, we create our map. We have to send it the map container, in this example, a div with the ID of, "map_canvas". Secondly, we pass it the map options we just went over. This is done by creating a new Map object.

```
map = new
google.maps.Map(document.getElementById("map_canvas"),
myOptions);
```

Below the initialize function you will see the DIV used to contain the map. This can be positioned like any DIV normally would. The sizing of the map will be inherited from the size of the DIV.

```
<div id="map_canvas" style="width: 900px; height:
800px;"></div>
```

The last bit of code in this example is the call to the initialize function. This is a good practice to call after your div has been created. Since we're using JavaScript, if you try to create the map before the container exists, it won't be able to create the map. There are other advanced methods to allow you some greater flexibility with this, but using this approach is extremely simple, and will not give you any errors.

```
initialize();
```

More Discussion
Now that we've created our first map, let's take a look at some of the options available. We defined the zoom, center, and the

mapTypeId. The first two should be pretty clear in setting the position and the zoom level.

As we progress through this book, we'll start using more of these to control a wider area of options, most notably the styles, allowing you to customize the style of every element on the map.

Hybrid: This map type displays a transparent layer of major streets on satellite images.

Roadmap: This map type displays a normal street map. This is most among the most common map display, as well as the default view for all any Google map.

Satellite: This map type displays satellite images. Roads will not be highlighted or labeled.

Terrain: This map type displays maps with physical features such as terrain and vegetation.

Chapter 2: Overlays

Now that you've been able to create your own map, it's time to start putting things into your map. The API classifies these things as overlays, something that sits on top of your map. I'll take you through some of the most common examples and show you how to create them, basic styling, and how to interact with them.

Markers and Info Windows

So what makes mapping so useful is being able to place something on that map and then getting some information on that place. In this chapter, we'll explore placing markers and info windows.

Markers

The tricky thing about creating a map marker is that it requires a longitude and latitude. Google can convert an address for you (a process known as geocoding), but it places a daily cap on these conversions to 2500. So if you started with a map of 100 markers that all needed their positions geocoded, after 25 page views, you would reach your cap limit, and your map would stop showing any markers.

Additionally geocoding your marker locations in every page load creates 100 unnecessary steps in rendering your page. Regardless of how small the processing time is, this creates more load time for the end user that could easily be avoided.

Ideally, you will want to store all of these geocoded locations in a database or a text file to cache the results. This can be a bit advanced for this example though, so I'll provide an already geocoded latitude and longitude pairing for Detroit.

There are also a number of services available online that will convert these points for you. Just do a search for something similar to, "find latitude and longitude of an address" and start looking at some of the options.

Working with our previous example, in the initialize function, you can create your first marker. Placing the code right below the call creating the map, you can insert the following.

```
var marker = new google.maps.Marker({
    position: new google.maps.LatLng(42.3316033749167, -
83.04630989280702),
    map: map,
    title: 'Detroit'
});
```

This call to the Google Maps API creates a new marker. We give it a position with the provided coordinates to place a marker on Detroit, and you attach it to the map object "map" that was created in the previous step. If you hover over the marker you will see the title of, "Detroit" appear.

If we wanted to style this up even more, we could create an animation to drop the markers into place. In the marker options, add the option, "animation: google.maps.Animation.DROP". Alternatively, you can also add a basic animation to have markers bounce until you stop them.

There are many more options in the documentation to customize your markers and interact with them. From changing the marker icon, setting the opacity, or even design an icon just like you would a polygon.

Info Windows
Now if we're looking to make this even more useful, you can add some popup text when you click on a marker. This popup text will be placed in a contained called an info window. To make things more

interesting, we'll add multiple markers, so we can look at how the info windows behave when we have multiple markers on the map.

First, we'll duplicate the markers, keeping unique variable names, giving them all slightly different locations. You'll see all of this done already in the example for this chapter.

Next we'll need to create an info window object. There are two distinct ways that you can use info windows that will fall entirely to your own preference. You can allow multiple info windows open at a time or one single info window at a time.

To create multiple info windows, below each marker add this code, and just change the marker name.

```
infowindow1 = new google.maps.InfoWindow();
listener = google.maps.event.addListener(marker1,
'click', function() {
   infowindow1.setContent("Info Window for Detroit!!");
   infowindow1.open(map,marker1);
});
```

In this example, you're creating a single info window object for each marker. You are then creating a listener for that marker. Upon clicking on the marker, it will set the info window content and make it visible at the position of the marker.

If this is repeated for each marker, giving the info window a unique name each time, it will allow you to have multiple info windows at a time. However, if you only want one info window open at a time, only create one info window object, and reuse that same variable (which you can see in the provided example). This works because the content is stored in the listener for each marker. Essentially, in this case, the same info window is used any time you click a marker. The position will assume the marker position you're clicking and the content will be assigned each time you click on the marker.

Removing Markers

If you are building something interactive and need to remove a marker that your page has generated, don't worry, this is also a very simple process.

```
Marker.setMap(null);
```

Changing it to a map that does not exist will remove the marker from the map. This also takes it out of the DOM, so the browser has less to manage. This is also the same process of removing a polygon or a polyline from the map.

Polygons

Now that you've learned how to put a marker on a map, you may want to start getting a bit more advanced. A common use I've had for mapping is mapping out an area. Whether it's tracing a state boundary, county zip or political boundaries, this is extremely useful, but it can definitely become a bit trickier.

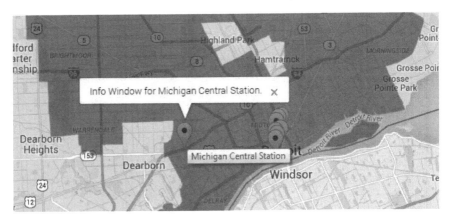

There are a few routes that can be taken for this. The easiest is if someone has already done all the leg work and mapped out an area that you need. These can be stored in KML files. Short for "Keyhole Markup Language", it is structured very similarly to XML. Very conveniently, the Google maps API has built in options to read KML in just two lines.

```
var kmzLayer = new
google.maps.KmlLayer('http://path.to/your.kml');
kmzLayer.setMap(map);
```

Fortunately, more and more KML data is being provided on various state and government sites for public use. From county level to state level, these premade KML files can be a big time saver. The downside is that you're locked into whatever is in the KML file and building out special interactions can be challenging.

If you have to do things the hard way like everyone else, you'll need to start mapping things out by hand. In the examples for this chapter, I provided a mapped out polygon for the city of Detroit. This is a more complex one since it includes multiple mapped out polygons, and is well over 1000 lines of coordinate data. While most polygons are a single shape, this one has multiple polygons in it, including an inner polygon that in effect creates a ring. This is a perfect example of a complex polygon.

In the example code, I create an empty array named "polygonCoordSet1". I then create five additional arrays named polyCoords0 through polyCoords4 which contain all of the coordinate data. Then I append the polyCoords arrays to the polygonCoordSet1 array. This is my array of coordinate sets now.

If you wanted a simple polygon, you could just create a single set such as polyCoords0 and use that, but in some instances, you may have to map a city like Detroit, which has an island separate from the main city, and two sections of the city which, even though they're internal, they do not belong to the city. In cases like these, you will map out each individual set, but they must all be sent together. This groups the outer areas, like the city and the island. It also creates an internal point that isn't mapped, which you can see in the example provided.

In this example, if we wanted to create our polygon, we could do so like this,

```
polygon1 = new google.maps.Polygon({
   paths: polygonCoordSet1,
   map: map
});
```

This will create a very plain looking polygon. If you want to add some common styling, you could do something like this,

```
polygon1 = new google.maps.Polygon({
  paths: polygonCoordSet1,
  map: map,
  strokeColor: '#00ff00',
  strokeOpacity: '0.8',
  strokeWeight: '1',
  fillColor: '#0000ff',
  fillOpacity: '0.5'
});
```

The coloring options work with normal RGB Hex that any web person should know. The weights and opacities have to be between 0 and 1. This makes things very easy to show visual data with a color key. Population, average household income, or any other easily found census data could be quickly shown in this method as long as you provide a key.

If you're looking to take things a little further, you're probably thinking about adding info windows again. Luckily you can, but you need just a little more code this time. Because a polygon doesn't have a single point, you need to capture a point. You could get the bounds and then the center of the polygon, or more commonly, get the mouse position where you clicked.

Since we're still working off the previous examples, we already have our info window object defined. We now have our polygon defined; all that's left is creating the listener for the polygon.

Placing this code after initializing your polygon will create an info window that will come up any time and anywhere you click on the polygon.

```
listener = google.maps.event.addListener(polygon1,
'click', function(event){
  infowindow.setContent("Welcome to Detroit, the home
of RoboCop.");
  infowindow.setPosition(event.latLng);
  infowindow.open(map);
});
```

This is the most complex way to create a polygon, because it gives the option for complex shapes. The Google Maps API does also offer more simple solutions if you are looking to create a rectangle or a circle, both with their own sets of options. These can be created very easily because they require minimal position information.

To size and position a more basic shape, rectangles require a bounds, the southwest and northeast latitude and longitude positions. These can be made as polygons, but this ensures they are as square as Google can make them.

```
rectangle = new google.maps.Rectangle(rectOptions);
```

Circles are a little different; they only require a center latitude and longitude position, and a radius.

```
circle = new google.maps.Circle(circleOptions);
```

Polylines

I wanted to save this for after the section on polygons intentionally simply because I wanted to keep things in order of how commonly I believe they are used, but by now you should also have a better understanding of things.

Much like polygons, polylines have multiple latitude and longitude points as well. The primary difference is, the positions don't try to close in like they do with polygons. Polylines could create a route, or even simulate a polygon, but essentially you're just drawing a path that has at a minimum, a start and an end.

For this section, let's say that we wanted to track the distribution of... just about anything. This would be a simple task. It would be a series of lines, each with the same starting latitude and longitude, followed by a different longitude and latitude.

In this example, let's create a function called, "addLine" that we can reuse.

```
function addLine(startlat, startlng, endlat, endlng){
    var line = new google.maps.Polyline({
        path: [new google.maps.LatLng(startlat, startlng),
new google.maps.LatLng(endlat, endlng)],
        map: map,
        geodesic: true,
        strokeOpacity: 0.8
    });
}
```

This code creates a new Polyline. The path in this example includes a starting position and an ending position, though you could continue adding more points. Each point being used in the polyline is a latitude / longitude object. The polyline is applied to the map we've been working with named, "map".

To keep things looking nice, I've set geodesic to true. This will curve the lines to simulate the curvature of the earth. The fastest way between points is always a straight line, but in a case like this, our straight lines are on a curved surface, and setting geodesic will visually show that by curving the line to match the curve of placing a round object on a flat surface.

Lastly, we set the strokeOpacity, to have s slight transparent effect. This isn't a requirement, but it does show some similarities between polygons and polylines. This is something you will see frequently; a lot of different types of objects may share similar attributes and characteristics.

Building from our initial examples, we can set our initial point as Detroit, with a latitude and longitude as "42.3316033749167" and "-83.04630989280702" respectfully. For the two ending points, you can choose these at random.

If you look at the example from this section, you will be able to see a series of lines coming out from Detroit and landing all over the state, country, and even the world. This is a cool way to show manufacturing partners, friends, places you've visited, or any kind of connection between two physical locations.

Chapter 3:
Taking advantage of the tools provided

Now that we've spent some time working on the basics, we should be ready to start having some real fun, giving our maps higher levels of functionality. Luckily, there are some ways to start adding a lot of functionality without adding so much work.

Geocoding: converting an address to a position

One of the most useful mapping services that Google provides in my opinion is the ability to geocode an address. This is the process of taking an address and trying to find it on the map and returning a latitude and longitude. When I first started getting serious about mapping, this was among the first tools I've written, and is probably the single most helpful tool I've ever made for mapping.

This is especially useful since having latitude and longitude pairs will map faster and more accurately than an address. Google also limits the number of addresses it will convert on a daily basis to 1,500. So when you start mapping out larger sets of data, you will want to geocode the addresses, then store the relative latitude and longitude pairing and use that going forward.

When it comes to geocoding, always try to have a complete address as you possibly can. It sounds like a no brainer, but if I search for Toledo, it doesn't know if I want Toledo, Ohio, or Toledo, Spain. If you're geocoding a bulk list of addresses, you'll be bound to get a few out-of-place markers because of this. Addresses aren't always consistent. 120 E. Fuller Drive and 120 Fuller may be the same address, but differences like this can trip up the system from time to time. In fact, when you're going for accuracy, it never hurts to include the city, state or zip code. Google does its best to find a match, but treat it like you're writing a letter, and you'll likely always find what you're looking for.

So now I'll walk you through building your own basic geocoder.

Typically I'll do this server side in another language because I find myself parsing spread sheets of data. However, when I'm in a crunch, I like to have a quick and simple look up tool.

This can all be done in three components: The Google Maps API include, some page structure to provide and receive the address and latitude and longitude pair, and a JavaScript function to make and process the request.

We'll start with our basic page structure, including the Google maps API JavaScript link.

```
<script type="text/javascript"
src="https://maps.googleapis.com/maps/api/js?v=3.exp&se
nsor=false"></script>
```

Next, in the <BODY> we'll include a basic structure. We're not going to focus on making it pretty, so we'll create a simple table to give it a bare minimum approach. This is a tool that I've always used only for personal use, so there isn't much need to make anything more attractive.

This includes the basics that we'll need for geocoding, an address field, a submit button to process the address, and a latitude and longitude field to display our results.

```
<table>
  <tr>
    <td>Address: </td>
    <td><input type="text" id="markerAddress"></td>
  </tr>
  <tr>
    <td>Latitude: </td>
```

```
    <td><input type="text" id="markerLat"></td>
  </tr>
  <tr>
    <td>Longitude: </td>
    <td><input type="text" id="markerLng"></td>
  </tr>
  <tr>
    <td colspan="2"><span
onClick="getAddressLatLng();">Geocode this
address</span></td>
  </tr>
</table>
```

Note the call in the last table row. We'll create that now and then walk you through it. This can be placed anywhere.

```
<script type="text/javascript">
function getAddressLatLng(){
  var geocoder = new google.maps.Geocoder();
  var address =
document.getElementById("markerAddress").value;
  geocoder.geocode( { 'address': address},
function(results, status) {
    if (status == google.maps.GeocoderStatus.OK) {
      var input = String(results[0].geometry.location);
      var latlngStr = input.substring(1,input.length-
1).split(',');
      document.getElementById("markerLat").value =
parseFloat(latlngStr[0]);
      document.getElementById("markerLng").value =
parseFloat(latlngStr[1]);
    } else {
      alert("Geocode was not successful: " + status);
    }
  });
}
</script>
```

First we define the geocoder.
```
var geocoder = new google.maps.Geocoder();
```

Next we're getting the address from the page structure.
```
var address =
document.getElementById("markerAddress").value;
```

15

Now for the interesting part, we begin the request for the latitude and longitude.

```
geocoder.geocode( { 'address': address},
function(results, status) {
```

This request will search anywhere in the world for the address provided. If you want to get more advanced, you can provide some parameters, such as the bounds (these are two latitude and longitude pairs representing a South West and North East boundary.

Once that is executed, if there are any results provided, it will execute a function.

Getting the return value is done here, making it a string. This will return a value similar to "(42.331427, -83.0457538)"

```
var input = String(results[0].geometry.location);
```

The next step for this example is splitting the string into separate fields.

```
var latlngStr = input.substring(1,input.length-
1).split(',');
```

Lastly, we assign the two values to the text fields.

```
document.getElementById("markerLat").value =
parseFloat(latlngStr[0]);
document.getElementById("markerLng").value =
parseFloat(latlngStr[1]);
```

While this is extremely helpful, it's not too practical for large volumes of data. When that becomes necessary I would suggest turning to something server side and automating your scripts.

It's also important to remember, unless you pay for Google's mapping services, you'll still be limited to 2500 conversions a day, something that may give you an error for seemingly no reason.

Map events and interactions

One path I've taken in the past that felt a little trendy was having a contact form where the user could pick their location instead of typing it. To complete this action, you click your location on the map. This method looked at where the user clicked on the map, and passed the latitude and longitude along as a parameter to a server. This is regularly used today in "I was here" applications.

This is done in a very similar fashion to how we opened the polygon info window.

```
google.maps.event.addListener(map, 'click',
function(event) {
  thisLatLng = event.latLng;

  marker.setPosition(thisLatLng);
  marker.setVisible(true);

  infowindow.setContent("You just clicked here:
"+thisLatLng);
  infowindow.open(map,marker);

  listener = google.maps.event.addListener(marker,
'click', function() {
    infowindow.open(map,marker);
  });

});
```

First things first: We create the listener for the map itself. As you can see from above, this listener responds to a right click anywhere on the map.

```
google.maps.event.addListener(map, 'rightclick',
function(event) {
```

Next we capture the latitude and longitude pairing.

```
thisLatLng = event.latLng;
```

In this example, we want to be helpful, so we place a marker where the user clicked. This is possible since we just captured the latitude and longitude of where the user clicked.

```
marker.setPosition(thisLatLng);
marker.setVisible(true);
```

Now we open an info window at the marker position. In this example we're just reporting a position visually to the end user. You could also load an iframe with the latitude and longitude pairing as a parameter or you could make an ajax call to the server. There are a lot of useful ways that you could implement this submission.

```
infowindow.setContent("You just clicked here:
"+thisLatLng");
infowindow.open(map,marker);
```

The final step is attaching a click listener for the marker and the info window. If the user closes the info window, this will let them open it back up by clicking on the marker.

```
listener = google.maps.event.addListener(marker,
'click', function() {
   infowindow.open(map,marker);
});
```

The Google Maps API has a sizeable list of event triggers. Clicks are just one of them. There's a full list of these interactions in the documentation, but they are all used in the same way. You'll create a listener for the map that listens for a specific event. In this example, we listened for a click, you can create listeners that are fired when you change the zoom, drag the map, or resize the map window. Having this level of interactivity is what makes the Google Maps API so powerful. Depending on your specific application, you may only ever need a few of these at a time, but there are options to do almost anything.

KML and GeoJSON

When it comes to mapping, there are a number of ways to get your data into a map. Two really great places to start focus around KML and GeoJSON. These are both incredibly efficient and can package all the features of a hand built map.

KML

Keyhole Markup Language is a great tool if you have access to it. Built with a similar structure to XML, KML files store latitude and longitude for polygons, markers, polylines, all of those great mapping features. It also houses extended information; you can put extra content in there. If you know anyone who's familiar with ArcGis mapping software, they'll be able to provide you with some great examples of KML files.

So why do I like KML so much? It's not too hard to find mapped out KML files already. If you hunt around long enough, you'll find a lot of various KML files being provided already. The government census site is a great place to start.

KML is also easy to implement; just two lines of code. In a map, just after initializing the map, try the following

```
var kmzLayer = new
google.maps.KmlLayer('http://www.slyscripting.com/downl
oads/chapter3c.kml');
kmzLayer.setMap(map);
```

This creates the KML layer, and the second line attaches it to the map. This method looks for a few default named fields in your KML file.

One thing to note while testing this is that Google will cache your KML file so you may not see the changes immediately. If you're playing around with this, you should add a cache busting parameter to the end, such as "chapter3c.kml?rev=1". This is great for performance, but can make testing a lot more difficult. To overcome this, having a query string that is easy to change (or randomly generated), will prevent caching when you have changing KML data or are in a development stage.

If you're curious about KML structure so that you can generate your own, Google provides some great documentation here, https://developers.google.com/kml/documentation/kml_tut

You can also search the web for it and find many working samples.

GeoJSON

GeoJSON has a very similar structure to KML and it offers almost all of the same functionality, but has a different format. For those who have been working with JavaScript for a while, you're likely familiar with JSON, which stands for JavaScript Object Notation. JSON is a very simple way to create an object with human readable attributes, which is typically used for transmitting. GeoJSON being a variation of JSON was created specifically by developers. It has defined attributes and documentation on creating points, polygons, and paths.

The code itself is very simple to implement.

```
map.data.loadGeoJson(yourcode.json');
```

As you can see above, the GeoJSON is loaded through the map.data object. This loads your GeoJSON into the maps data layer, which also allows you to manipulate that information on the fly. Just scanning the documentation, you have easy access to set styles, loop through individual entries, and add/remove entries. My favorite of this is the ability to export the data layer to GeoJSON. This is particularly useful if you're creating something an in Admin interface that will be typically only viewed by normal users. This allows you to create an output that won't need as much processing as it would if you were creating every point by hand.

What's the difference?

From the outside, these two are extremely similar. Aside from some differences in their actual structure, they are able to create the same things. The difference comes into play when you look at the interactivity. For example, KML allows for a lot more pre-defined styling and interaction, where GeoJSON requires that to be done in your code after it's been loaded into your map. Both options have their advantages in how they're processed. Picking which format you'd like to use will likely boil down to your individual application, what format just feels more comfortable to you, or if you're using a 3rd party data set, they'll likely make that decision for you.

Chapter 4:
Fusion Tables

I wanted to give fusion tables their own section because they really are their own facet of mapping.

Let's start with these tables, what are they? Fusion Tables are essentially single table databases hosted through Google docs. As a result, they have incredibly fast load times when you use them in conjunction with a Google map. They also provide you with sample code so if you aren't comfortable with creating maps just yet, this can provide you with a nearly out-of-the-box solution.

I won't go into how to create a Google account. Odds are, you already have an account with one of the top websites on the internet.

Once signed into Google, access your Google Drive, and create a new Fusion Table.

From here you can import a document, including KML, or you can create a document by hand. For this lesson, import the KML file from the previous chapter.

Once it's uploaded you will see that it stores polygon data as well as coordinate data in location field types. You can even view the fusion table as a map. Fusion Tables offer you a great amount of capability without needing to know a lot of the ins and outs of mapping. You can assign images to markers, or set up rules for marker icons based on a field. You can do the same with polygons. You can also customize the info windows based on the available content. The only limitation here is that you can only provide what you have. If you need to show information based on a calculation, you'll need to apply it to the table. Also, if you'd like to show content based on certain conditions. For example, if a field has a value of zero, don't bother reporting it, there's no way to do that.

With that said, the fast loading times and ability to kick out a map with little mapping knowledge is typically worth the trade off for simple projects that just need to go live "right now".

Once you've uploaded your KML file, or created a fusion table, or even found a handy publicly accessible fusion table (there are many of them out there), we can start creating our fusion table based map! To enable it for mapping, you must also share your map as public or unlisted.

In this example, we'll be mapping out 5,753 Class C liquor license locations in Michigan. This information is all publically available online, and was geocoded using the Google Maps API and then formatted into a KML file and uploaded to become a fusion table. You may notice that some of the points are scattered across the country and the globe. This highlights the point that well-formatted addresses are pretty important. Since for this example, I just wanted quantity, I didn't worry too much about their physical locations, even if they've been incorrectly geocoded.

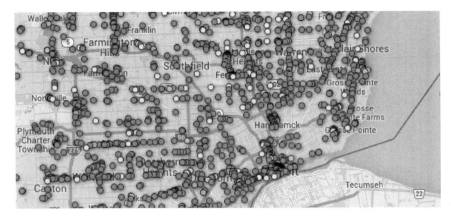

It's important to notice the load times. When dealing with fusion tables, Google will pre-render everything. Even though you lose some of the interactive options you may want, when you're dealing with massive amounts of data, this may give you a working option that you don't have when loading the same data locally.

Building off of the previous examples, once we initialize our map, we add the code for the fusion table layer:

```
layer = new google.maps.FusionTablesLayer({
  map: map,
  query: {
    select: "col5",
    from: "16n1-vGtoWcm9Va_plduPf0x0TiAVG27owe0XX-w",
    where: ""
  },
  options: {
    styleId: 2,
    templateId: 2
  }
});
```

Above you can see that we have now created our fusion table layer in the first line, then in the second line assigned it to the map we already initialized.

If you're familiar with SQL, then queries should feel fairly natural. This is essentially selecting something from a table. If there are any conditions on that select, they can be performed. In this example, the table ID comes from the fusion table itself.

Lastly, we can see the options for the table. This carries over marker styles and info window templates that may have been created in the fusion table document while accessing it from your Google Drive.

The Limitations: You cannot use more than five fusion tables in a map. If your data is fairly spaced out between multiple tables, you will need to condense it. You are also limited to the first 100,000 rows of data in your tables. The rest are simply not displayed. While these are realistic limitations, the trade-offs for speed and efficiency are still very appealing.

Chapter 5:
Ground Overlays (graphical overlays)

Every now and then, you'll have a project where you find a need to drop an image over a map. In most instances, a polygon or polylines are a preferred option because of their interactive options, but they don't fit every scenario and can reduce performance when they're too large. Luckily adding an image to a map is a pretty simple task with Ground Overlays. This is where you can take an image and attach it to a map based on latLng points for positioning. For this project we'll pick something simple, a historical map overlay. To make this one really authentic, we'll want to overlay a historical map over current day Michigan to show a past and present comparison.

Graphical overlays allow you to place an image on top of a map, and this can be done with any image. Unlike creating html overlays, these images are attached to the map. As you move the map around, the image will move with it, since it's attached to coordinate positions. As you zoom in and out, the image will zoom in and out with you, so you'll want to try to use a high resolution image.

Creating your ground overlay can be condensed into a single line, but breaking it out makes it a lot easier to read. When creating a ground overlay, you have three parameters: your image, the latitude and longitude bounds, and lastly, the map options. We can use the included image in the example.

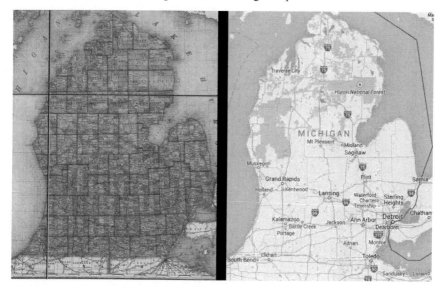

The first step is creating our bounds for the map. These aren't exact coordinates, but for a map that is over 150 years old they should be pretty close. Bounds as a refresher create a rectangle when you provide the latLng positions for the southwest and northeast positions.

The second step is providing our image. Google will scale this image to fit the bounds you've provided. It is then placed inside of the map for viewing.

Lastly, you can add some optional parameters. Ground Overlays don't have too many options, just the map on which it will display, the overlay opacity, and whether or not it's clickable.

```
var overlayBounds = new google.maps.LatLngBounds(new
google.maps.LatLng(41.57436, -87.36328), new
google.maps.LatLng(45.79816, -82.08984));
var overlayOptions = {
  map: map
}
var overlay = new
google.maps.GroundOverlay("1885map.jpg", overlayBounds,
overlayOptions);
```

Since this is a historical map, we'll also give you a nice ability to see the before and after shots. To do this, we need a trigger, which we'll do with a simple mouseOver for the div. To keep things simple, I'm going to use jQuery to aid in this.

The most obvious thing we need to do is include jQuery, then we need to include our div to track. We could use the map container itself, but that may create some poor usability.

```
<script src="http://code.jquery.com/jquery-
latest.min.js" type="text/javascript"></script>
<div class="trackMe" style="width: 900px; height: 40px;
background-color:#cccccc;">…</div>
```

Next, we'll include our jQuery code to control the visibility. I won't go too much into the details here, since jQuery isn't the focus and is a very mainstream tool. The main purpose we're achieving is getting the current position of the mouse inside of the "trackMe" div. Then we're able to divide that position by the overall width, and turn that into a percent. That percent is what we're able to use to control the opacity of our overlay. For simplicity, we'll define a width of 900px to our "trackMe" div to match our map container.

```
$(document).ready(function() {
  $('.trackMe').mousemove(function(e) {
    var offset = $(this).offset();
    var xpos = (e.pageX - offset.left);
    var thisWidth = 900;
    var pct = Math.round((xpos/thisWidth)*100)/100;
    var ipct = Math.abs(Math.round(((xpos-
thisWidth)/thisWidth)*100)/100);
    overlay.setOpacity(ipct);
  });
});
```

Now as you move the mouse from left to right you should see the overlay fade out of view.

Some great applications for this

There are a lot of times that ground overlays are useful. Above is a perfect example, but taking things further, you could show a map of a sports stadium and make an interactive map of foul balls, or allow people to click where they were sitting on opening day of a game. Taking this up to a larger scale could be just as easy if you wanted to show the geographical changes that earthquakes, flooding, or even volcanoes can have on an area.

If you're creating a "coverage area" map, I mentioned that being able to quickly geocode a single address saves time in a pinch, it can also help with efficiency. If you need to map out every zip code in your state, sometimes finding that latitude and longitude data can be tedious at best. Adding an image overlay can let you achieve the same goals with a fraction of the time involvement. It can also keep things loading smoother since it isn't mapping out the thousands of map positions. This is an ideal approach if you're mapping out something like census data based on geographic regions or even something as simple as voting districts. You lose some of the interactive options but depending on the size of the area (because of the strain it can put on the browser) or time restraints a graphical ground overlay may be the perfect solution.

Chapter 6:
Street View

Street view is one of the cooler features so far offered by Google Maps. This allows any user to take a look visually at a map as if they were walking on the street. To show a nice application of this, imagine we are looking for people to bid on public art sponsorships. As part of this, we'll need to be able to show perspective bidders where these projects are located and give them a nice in-person view of them. Fortunately for us, Google is constantly expanding the coverage areas for street view.

We'll start by creating our map like normal. This time we'll also add a number of markers for public areas (I've included these in the example). I won't get into the marker creation, but I will point out that we need some additional steps in this process. We'll need to create a container for our street view to show up just like we do for our map. For this example, let's create this inside of the map. *Make sure that you don't clear the map container content.*

```
<div id="map_canvas" style="width: 900px; height:
800px;">
    <div id="streetView"></div>
</div>
```

We'll also need to add some special styling to this to make sure it looks normal. This will let us place a nice little window in the bottom right corner of our map for our street views.

```
<style type="text/css">
#map_canvas{
    position:relative;
}

#streetView{
    position:absolute;
    width:300px;
    height:200px;
    bottom:50px;
    right:50px;
    z-index:100;
}
</style>
```

Creating our street view. Since we're pairing these with markers in this example, we'll need to create our markers for predefined locations that have street view available.

First you see our marker. This is created just as the rest of the markers we've made.

```
var marker3 = new google.maps.Marker({
    position: new google.maps.LatLng(42.337176, -
83.04939200000001),
    map: map,
    title: 'Russell A. Alger Memorial Fountain'
});
```

Now we can start creating our street view object. This takes two parameters; our HTML container, and the street view options. Since we are using such a limited space for the street view, it is best that we disable all of the window overlays that would typically be in position.

Position: The options include a position of a longitude and latitude pairing. Since these are related to the markers, we are able to get the same position of the marker.

Pov: This is where we define our street Point-Of-View. This only has three options.

Heading: The direction that the camera will face, in degrees, relative to true north.

Pitch: The camera pitch is the angel that you are looking out from, relative to the Google vehicle that took the images.

Zoom: Exactly what it sounds like, the level of zoom on the street view.

disableDefaultUI: This is how you remove all of the street view User Interface controls. These can all be done individually.

```
var panoramaOptions3 = {
  position: marker3.getPosition(),
  pov: {
    heading: -108.78144080577084,
    pitch: 5.175438782372692,
    zoom: 1.9900000000000002
  },
  disableDefaultUI: true
};
```

Now we're able to create our street view for this object. Since we aren't making it active by default, we won't attach it to the map yet like we normally would with anything else we've made.

```
var panorama3 = new
google.maps.StreetViewPanorama(document.getElementById(
'streetView'),panoramaOptions3);
```

Finally we set up the listener for the marker. This listener will set the street view to attach to the map when you click on it. Since the listener already has its container that doesn't need to be hidden or removed. Once it's attached to the map, it becomes active.

```
listener = google.maps.event.addListener(marker3,
'click', function() {
  map.setStreetView(panorama3);
});
```

Taking it a step further

One thing that we could do to take this a step further is give it a reporting element. If we know the general area of something but aren't for sure, we can drag it into position then capture the position and point of view elements that we'd need, allowing you to give your street views more precise starting positions.

To do this we'll add an additional textarea component to the bottom of our page to display the results.

```
<textarea id="streetViewCode" style="width: 900px;
height: 240px;"></textarea>
```

Now we need our listener. Whenever the point of view is changed for our street view, this will generate code to create a street view window looking exactly where the live window is looking.

```
listener = google.maps.event.addListener(panorama3,
'pov_changed', function() {
  var panoPov = panorama3.getPov();
  var panoPos = panorama3.getPosition();
  var streetViewCode =
document.getElementById("streetViewCode");
  content = "var panoramaOptions = {\n";
  content += " position: new
google.maps.LatLng("+panoPos.lat()+",
"+panoPos.lng()+"),\n";
  content += " pov: {\n";
  content += "    heading: -108.78144080577084,\n";
  content += "    pitch: 5.175438782372692,\n";
  content += "    zoom: 1.9900000000000002\n";
  content += " },\n";
  content += " disableDefaultUI: true\n";
  content += "};\n";
  content += "var panorama = new
google.maps.StreetViewPanorama(document.getElementById(
'streetView'),panoramaOptions);";
  streetViewCode.value = content;
});
```

A bit more information

Street view being as unique a feature as it is, does allow for a few additional options that didn't fit this example. The first being a hugely convenient one is the ability to check whether or not street view exists at a location.

Testing a location can be done by providing a specific panorama ID using the function "getPanoramaId()" or providing a latLng object using the "getPanoramaByLocation()" function. This is a useful option any time you're automating functionality.

In addition to testing if a street view exists, you can also define your own panorama by defining the option, "panoProvider". This will allow you to call a user defined function, where you can eventually set your own tiles. These tiles are simple images that allow you to base the selection on the zoom and the x/y position. This might be a particularly useful feature if you were trying to show proposed build plans for a site that didn't exist yet.

Chapter 7: Searching

It's no real secret, Google is a search giant. Since they first started back in 1998, they've managed to revolutionize how the world finds data. Starting by indexing webpages, they've grown to add almost everything we can think of. This is hugely beneficial to mapping since one of their focuses have been indexing businesses.

As things have moved forward, being able to search for a location has been added to maps. This adds new applications for interaction and data extraction.

For this chapter, we'll build a safety map. Based on the current map window, we'll identify all police departments, fire stations, and hospitals.

The first step in adding search into our maps will be using the places library. This is specified in the call to our API. Without adding the places library, none of this will work.

```
<script
src="https://maps.googleapis.com/maps/api/js?v=3.exp&li
braries=places"></script>
```

Initializing our search is pretty straight forward. Following the same structure we've been using, we'll just need to place this inside of our initializing function.

```
thesePlaces = document.getElementById('thesePlaces');

var service = new
google.maps.places.PlacesService(map);

google.maps.event.addDomListener(map, 'bounds_changed',
function(){
  var request = {
    bounds: map.getBounds(),
    types: ['police', 'fire_station', 'hospital']
  };
  service.nearbySearch(request, theResults);
});
```

In the code above, the first thing to note is this is placed in a listener. Because we're restricting our results to the bounds of the map, we need to have a map that's already initialized, otherwise, our bounds will come back undefined, and our search will not work.

To perform the actual search, we will need to create our Places object. From here, we're able to continue making new requests.

The actual request in this example searches only the bounds and three types of locations as defined by Google. The documentation gives a wide range of options for this, from searching a radius, keywords, required set of text in a places name or even requiring the place to be open right now.

Once this has performed the search, the callback function "theResults" is called and passed three parameters for the results, the status, and the pagination.

The status parameter is particularly important since if there's an error in the search or no results, we won't be trying to process results that don't exist.

Once we know we are clear to process the results, all that's left is looping through the results and placing the markers on the map. Google does provide a nice degree of data along with their places, so this is a very simple process.
Each place as you can see below already has information associated with it containing the image, name and position.

```
function theResults(results, status, pagination) {
  if(status !=
google.maps.places.PlacesServiceStatus.OK){
    return; //if we didn't get any results
  }
  for(var i = 0, place; place = results[i]; i++) {
    var image = {
      url: place.icon
    };
    var marker = new google.maps.Marker({
      map: map,
      icon: image,
      title: place.name,
      position: place.geometry.location
    });
    thesePlaces.innerHTML += place.name + '<br>';
  }
}
```

This could be easily extended to include info windows with more information, but you are limited to what information is returned. Depending on the application, this might be an ideal way to add a directions link or a way to add it to your favorites.

If you're looking to take your searches further, you are also able to change the search rankings and go through search result paginations. In addition you can get a places details, which will require yet another call back function. The benefit to this is the amount of data you can provide. This can include the address, phone number, photos, price levels, ratings, their site, and much more. If you're making an interactive tool, this is a perfect place to start.

Like anything else with Google Maps, there are always some limitations. Data caps and inaccurate data are the first two that come to mind. With the search feature, you're tied to their search, so you may want a hospital, but you'll have to filter through some medical marijuana clinics in your results first. If you don't have a frame work populated with data already though, this solution is hard to compete with.

Chapter 8:
Making it look good

One thing I've learned in my time as a web developer is that people don't care too much about what you're producing until it looks good. I could put the formula for turning lead to gold online, but if the button is the wrong shade of blue, no one will want to use it. Ok, maybe that's an exaggeration... Maybe...

This is where we can start going pretty in depth on everything since Google allows a pretty decent level of customizable controls.

Adding HTML into Info Windows

This is probably the first place that anyone will want to start since it's among the most frequently used area for maps.

The best thing to know here is, info windows can receive HTML. This is great for a wide array of styling. If you're placing a lot of information in an info window, this lets you really take control of the appearance.

Info windows will inherit styling from your own page. Typically this is great, since that's exactly what you would want them to do. Every now and then you'll run into some weird issues.

If you have a page that loads any of it's styling dynamically, then the map may render before the styling can be rendered. This will create a problem and your info windows might not be large enough, among other issues. Luckily you can remedy this by placing your styling inline in the info windows. I won't go too in-depth with this, since everyone reading this should know how to use inline styles, but I will include this in the examples, I also wanted to make sure this was addressed in the hope that it saves some of you a fair amount of time in figuring out why your info windows aren't coming out right.

This is useful because you can create basic HTML layout and style them with CSS.

Custom icons and positioning

One of the first things I wanted to do when I started with creating mappable objects was having my own custom icon images. I felt like it gave my maps a nice sense of ownership. As it turns out, this is relatively easy to achieve.

From our previous examples of creating a marker, we'll start adding some customizations to this marker.

```
var image = {
  url: 'http://www.nogumallowed.com/images/icon15.png',
  origin: new google.maps.Point(0,0),
  size: new google.maps.Size(10, 10, 'pixels',
'pixels'),
  scaledSize: new google.maps.Size(10, 10, 'pixels',
'pixels'),
  anchor: new google.maps.Point(5, 5)
};

var marker1 = new google.maps.Marker({
  position: new google.maps.LatLng(42.3316033749167, -
83.04630989280702),
  map: map,
  title: 'Detroit',
  icon: image
});
```

In this example, we use almost identical code to before, but we create the "image" variable, and add it to the marker options. There are a lot of fields for the image, so let's take a look at them.

This specifies a path to the image.

```
url: ' http://www.slyscripting.com/downloads/user-
icon.png',
```

This is done by default, but I wanted to include it to make a good point. In making things more efficient, google frequently uses sprites. Sprites are images with multiple images in them. This is a web trick used for speeding up load times. Since combining the images reduces file size and load times as a result, you can specify the location of the image. If you had two 10x10 images combined vertically for a sprite, and you wanted to select the second image within the image, you would set an origin of 0,10, then below, you would select a size of 10,10. However, if you're image is only one image (which it likely will be in most cases), you can leave this out, or just use it as I have below.

```
origin: new google.maps.Point(0,0),
```

This specifies the image area. If you have single image, then you just put in the image dimensions. If you are using a sprite, then you specify the area you want to select for the sprite.

```
size: new google.maps.Size(10, 10, 'pixels'),
```

This is pretty useful if you're using the same image, but changing the size to reflect something else visually, such as... "The number of times I've been to this location". This will stretch the selected image area to the dimensions you provide. In this example, we aren't stretching it all, so it didn't need to be specified.

```
scaledSize: new google.maps.Size(10, 10, 'pixels'),
```

Lastly, this is pretty useful. The anchor is the position on the marker that lines up on the map. If you are using a round image, and have a polyline connected to this point, then you would want to have that polyline connect to the center of the circle. So in this instance, we have a 10x10 image, we set the anchor to the center of the image, at 5,5.

```
anchor: new google.maps.Point(5, 5)
```

Adding HTML into maps

Google really does provide a lot of options and controls to do a lot of stuff, but every now and then you'll run into a map control that you know how to code, but the Google Maps API doesn't give you a nice neat way to add it to the map. You might also create a map with a fairly specific purpose, but you need some extended functionality. Luckily, you can place HTML on top of a map allowing you to really add some new options.

We'll start with a very basic one, a reset button. A simple button that if you change the zoom and scroll all over the map, this will let you hit a button in the top right corner to take you back to your initial starting point.

I'll leave the styling up to you for your button, but I'll include some in the sample to get you started, just remember that you'll have to set the z-index, otherwise the map will sit on top of anything you leave in the div.

The first thing we do is create our button. Nested in the div container for the map. This includes a function to set the current map settings, and if you look close, you'll recognize the latitude, longitude, and a 3rd parameter for the zoom level.

```
<div id="map_canvas" style="width: 900px; height:
800px;">
      <div class="resetButton"
onClick="setCurrentMapSettings('42.33355446826103', '-
83.04900283065797', 15)">Reset</div>
</div>
```

Now naturally, we need to place our "setCurrentMapSettings" function. This is a very simple three line function. The first line creates a longitude and latitude object, the second line moves the map to that point, and the third line sets the zoom level.

```
function setCurrentMapSettings(latitude, longitude,
zoom){
   var myLatLng = new google.maps.LatLng(latitude,
longitude);
   map.panTo(myLatLng);
   map.setZoom(zoom);
}
```

The last piece involved is telling the map initializer not to over-write or replace the containing div content. Adding the option, "noClear: true" will make sure that anything that was placed in the div initially, will remain in the div.

```
noClear: true
```

This is an incredibly useful ability, and while it doesn't require any direct API knowledge, it does allow you to create mapping interfaces in the very simplified way. While our example was a very simple one, the same methods could be used to create a slide out options panel that allow you to toggle all sorts of settings from map types, to customizing tools for map markers and polygons.

Styling the map itself

The first time I had a request for this, I wasn't even sure that it was possible. I see Google maps all over the web, all the time, and I've seen some of them do some particularly creative things, but I wasn't sure that I had ever seen a Google map that had been styled so that certain elements were hidden, and others were given different colors or opacity. As it turns out, this was very possible, and a great way to really drive home the point of a map.

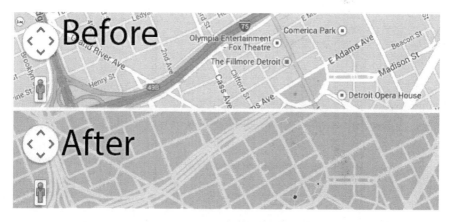

Luckily, Google does give you a decent level of customization, but the documentation on what is what, is a little vague, so it takes some playing around with.

Let's start simple, we can create something a little artistic, showing a basic transit layout.

```
var mapStyles = [{featureType: "all",
  elementType: "labels",
  stylers: [{visibility: 'off'}]},

  {featureType: "poi",
  elementType: "all",
  stylers: [{visibility: 'off'}]},

  {featureType: "road",
  elementType: "all",
  stylers: [{visibility: 'simplified'},{color:
'#DAFFB2'}]},

  {featureType: "landscape",
  elementType: "all",
  stylers: [{visibility: 'on'},{color: '#99D5F1'}]},

  {featureType: "water",
  elementType: "all",
  stylers: [{color: '#2831FF'}]}];

var styledMapType = new
google.maps.StyledMapType(mapStyles);

map.mapTypes.set('customStyleID', styledMapType);
map.setMapTypeId('customStyleID');
```

This map has a bit more code, but giving it a closer look, you will see that it's primarily all styling code. Styling sometimes has a bit more 'ins and outs', but if you're familiar with CSS, then you should be accustomed to this already. The positive side of this is, you can apply fairly specific styling to something on the map, while the rest of the map will maintain a default styling.

The first thing we do in this is create our map style options. This can be seen in the variable "mapStyles". In this section of code, we identify various mapping attributes and set options for them such as visibility, color, etc. This is handled in an extremely similar way to CSS, where there are parent elements and child elements. You can set all "Roads" to invisible, but then "road.local" to visible, and apply additional styling to them only on this level.

```
var mapStyles = [{featureType: "all",
```

The next step is making this into an actual style object recognized by the Google API.

```
var styledMapType = new
google.maps.StyledMapType(mapStyles);
```

After this is done, we have to create a mapType ID so that it can be applied to the map. This allows us to assign a string to it to identify it, which will lastly, allow us to set that map style to the map.

```
map.mapTypes.set('customStyleID', styledMapType);
map.setMapTypeId('customStyleID');
```

If you're looking for an extremely useful playground for this, then I suggest checking out the styled maps wizard http://gmaps-samples-v3.googlecode.com/svn/trunk/styledmaps/wizard/index.html

Heat Maps

Heat maps allow you in a visual way demonstrate the density of markers on a map. This is a great way to map out the density of restaurants across a state, for example. Heat maps also allow you to assign weights to each marker, so that if you instead wanted to track the value of homes, you could set weights appropriately to show the densities of higher priced homes.

In creating a heat map, you'll need a lot of markers. In the example provided, I've attached a file with 5000+ markers in it, as we'll need a lot of areas to show the density just right. This is a lot, but it will help me touch on a point later on as well.

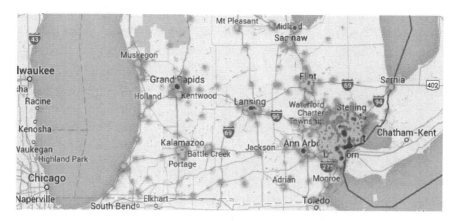

Creating a localized heat map

Heat maps require an additional visualization library, so you have to make sure you're calling this in the API request. It's one of those things that is really easy to overlook.

```
<script type="text/javascript"
src="https://maps.googleapis.com/maps/api/js?v=3.exp&se
nsor=false&libraries=visualization"></script>
```

Now we can create our heatmap data. I'm doing this with a straight forward array of lat/lng points.

```
var heatmapData = [
new google.maps.LatLng(42.2692640, -83.1818850),
new google.maps.LatLng(42.3351391, -83.0423178),
new google.maps.LatLng(42.4330141, -83.0415078),
...
];
```

Once we've initialized the map, we create our heat map object

```
var heatmap = new
google.maps.visualization.HeatmapLayer({
  data: heatmapData,
  radius: 50
});
```

If you look at the parameters, you'll see I set the heat map data to the data set we just created. I also assigned it a radius of 50 to make sure that it was visible. This is a number you can feel free to play around with.

Lastly, we attach it to the map.

```
heatmap.setMap(map);
```

Creating a fusion table heat map

Now one thing you may notice while zooming or loading the page is that it takes a bit longer for the load time. That's simply because of the mass amounts of points that it has to track. Not too long ago, heat maps were offered ONLY for fusion tables. Consequently, creating a fusion table heat map is incredibly easy, and will load at a far greater speed.

Creating the code is almost identical to creating any fusion table; just include the heat map option.

```
layer = new google.maps.FusionTablesLayer({
  map: map,
  heatmap: { enabled: true },
  query: {
    select: "col5",
    from: "16n1-vGtoWcm9Va_plduPf0x0TiAVG27owe0XX-w",
    where: ""
  },
  options: {
    styleId: 2,
    templateId: 2
  }
});
```

The differences in localizing and using a fusion table

Using a fusion table will greatly improve the speed of anything compared to keeping it local. This example was done with 5000+ markers. Imagine mapping out counties in a state. This could take up to a minute to load locally in a browser. However if you load this from a fusion table, it will load without any noticeable lag time. In cases like this, the decision may be made for you, since user experience is always likely a top concern.

If you are working with a smaller amount of data, then you may opt to keep things localized. While you will lose the speed and efficiency of a fusion table, you gain far greater control over the data for customization. Additionally, this will save you the trouble of constantly re-uploading your work if this is a developing project. Both options have benefits, and deciding which one has the biggest advantage will typically come down to the needs of the specific project.

Chapter 9:
Additional Features

This is where we can start having some fun with things. We've got the very basics down, and we can start diving into the more powerful tools and options. Weather, traffic, directions, are some of the examples of the things that give your maps more of a purpose and take it from a supporting feature on a site to a core component.

These services still have a lot of the common limitations as Google places caps on the number of times a day that you can use certain services for free. For general use though, you'll be fine.

Finding browser locations

This is something that is becoming more and more common. Finding a user's location based on their browser is commonly referred to as geolocating. This is far from a perfect system, but still shows a TON of promise. It also gives you a great start on things if you can detect a user's location as opposed to having them have to waste the time to punch it in themselves. This can help you develop code that is intuitive to a user's current location.

This will work differently on all devices as they all have different methods of obtaining a current location. Cell phones might get this from GPS or from cell towers. They might also have the location cached.

You will also need to consider browser support as a whole. As noted this is done using HTML5. Currently, browser support is available across the major browsers, and IE 9+.

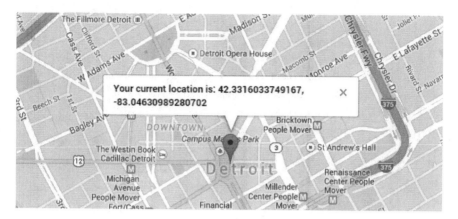

In the example below, we'll look for the browser location, then send the users position to our initialize function.

```
if(navigator.geolocation) {
  navigator.geolocation.getCurrentPosition(
    function(position) {
      initialize(position.coords.latitude,
position.coords.longitude);},
    function(position) {
      initialize('42.503977469175325', '-
83.44762200561524');},
    {maximumAge:60000, timeout:5000,
enableHighAccuracy:true}
  );
}
else{
  initialize('42.503977469175325', '-
83.44762200561524');
}
```

The first thing we're doing is making sure this function is supported by the browser. If it isn't, then it's good to have a fall-back plan. This will default to a pre-defined location if we can't find a location.
```
if(navigator.geolocation) {
```

Next, the code may look a bit complex, but we're running a couple of functions as our parameters. This is a common practice, so this

47

shouldn't throw anyone off, but it can make it a bit messy to read. The browser function to get the current position has three parameters defining how to execute upon success, an error, and what options to include. If we find the location, then we send it to our initialize function, if we fail to find the location, we will send a default location, the same as when the functionality does not exist. The last set is the function options. These are very important, and should not be left off.

```
navigator.geolocation.getCurrentPosition(success,
error, options)
```

When making a request for a browser location it's important to know that this request will not time out on its own. The fail will not automatically call itself unless it hits an actual error while retrieving the location.

```
{maximumAge:60000, timeout:5000,
enableHighAccuracy:true});
```

These three options are the only options available currently.
timeout: This is exactly as it sounds, the amount of time before failing while retrieving a location in milliseconds.
maximumAge: If you are performing these requests on multiple pages, then this is very useful, this will use a cached device location as long as it doesn't exceed the specified age. This can improve the process times significantly.
enableHighAccuracy: This indicates that if a device can get a more accurate position then it will try to do so. Devices with GPS chips will likely be used if set to true. It should be noted that this will increase load times, and potentially use more power from the device.

You should also beware of strange behavior with this. Sometimes internet services are bounced across the country (this can be especially true if your work has a large corporate infrastructure), and cell phones can bounce off of many towers. Coincidentally, I've seen strange behavior before when a site asks a user for permission to use their location and it is denied. This is still a relatively young browser ability, but I anticipate it will become stronger and stronger as browser updates are pushed out in the future, especially for use on mobile devices.

Direction based services

In my opinion, this is one of the most commonly used features when developing applications for Google maps. If you're building a site that indexes restaurants then this is a great application of the Google Maps. Odds are you are already showing a map on the page, so the next logical step is to show directions.

You can show these from a fixed location, or use what we learned in our previous example to show the directions from the user's current location.

```javascript
function initialize(lat, lng) {

var directionsDisplay = new google.maps.DirectionsRenderer();
var directionsService = new google.maps.DirectionsService();

var myOptions = {
   zoom: 15,
   center: new google.maps.LatLng(42.33160, -83.04630),
   mapTypeId: google.maps.MapTypeId.ROADMAP
}
map = new
google.maps.Map(document.getElementById("map_canvas"),
myOptions);

directionsDisplay.setMap(map);
directionsDisplay.setPanel(document.getElementById("mymapdire
ction"));

var request = {
   origin: new google.maps.LatLng(lat, lng),
   destination: new google.maps.LatLng(destlat, destlng),
   travelMode: google.maps.TravelMode.DRIVING
};

directionsService.route(request, function(response, status) {
   if (status == google.maps.DirectionsStatus.OK) {
     directionsDisplay.setDirections(response);
     var leg = response.routes[ 0 ].legs[ 0 ];
   }
   else{
     //you hit your quota, time to show a default marker
     var marker = new google.maps.Marker({
       position: new google.maps.LatLng(42.33160, -83.046309),
       map: map,
       title: 'Detroit'
     });
   }
});
}
```

Once the initialize function is called with the latitude and longitude pair, the first thing we do is initialize our directions object. There are two of them, one for the map, and one for the written out directions.

```
var directionsDisplay = new
google.maps.DirectionsRenderer();
var directionsService = new
google.maps.DirectionsService();
```

Next we set the destination latitude and longitude pair. In this example, this is Detroit. This could just as easily be a restaurant that you are mapping some directions to. In this example we are providing these as a hard coded option. If you applied some server side coding, this could very easily be placed dynamically.

```
var destlat = '42.33160337493167';
var destlng =   '-83.04630989280702';
```

The next block of code you should be very familiar with by now. This is where we create and initialize our map.

Once we've initialized our directions object, we can set it to the map.

```
directionsDisplay.setMap(map);
```

This is the same case for our written direction. We can set these to display in a div below the map.

```
directionsDisplay.setPanel(document.getElementById("mym
apdirection"));
```

Our request is created here. We give it out starting points and destination points. This is nothing more than just a request set.

```
var request = {
  origin: new google.maps.LatLng(lat, lng),
  destination: new google.maps.LatLng(destlat,
destlng),
  travelMode: google.maps.TravelMode.DRIVING
};
```

Here we take that request set and turn it into the actual directions. If we have a successful request, then we pass the response (the directions) to the directions object.

```
directionsService.route(request, function(response,
status) {
  if (status == google.maps.DirectionsStatus.OK) {
    directionsDisplay.setDirections(response);
  }
```

In the event that the request has failed, we show the end point by itself instead of an empty map.

```
else{
    //you hit your quota, time to show a default marker
    var marker = new google.maps.Marker({
        position: new
google.maps.LatLng(42.3316033749167, -
83.04630989280702),
        map: map,
        title: 'Detroit'
    });
}
```

It's good to make a note that currently, you are allowed 2,500 requests per day. In this example, the request for the map display, as well as the written directions request both count against you. In this example, we would only be allowed 1,250 page requests before reaching the cap and needing to upgrade to a paid account with Google. Unfortunately, this isn't a very high number. That is why it's always good to have the fall back to display only the single marker point to avoid having an empty map show up.

In this example, we use the default markers and info windows; it is also possible to customize the markers for this as well as the info windows. If you look at the corresponding example file, you will see this done. The code is very similar to everything we've done so far, but I didn't include it in here simply because the example code would start to grow rapidly.

Taking it Further
This example maps a path that may always be different every time it's loaded. If you are going to be giving directions between two fixed points (for example, highlighting a race course), you should cache your results. Each request will have "legs" containing start and end points that can be mapped. Running the directions once, then capturing these points to make markers and polylines afterward will avoid making the request to the API as well as avoid the capping limits imposed on this service.

Traffic and weather maps

Now that we're starting to dive into mapping around the individual, it may only be natural to start including traffic stats or weather.

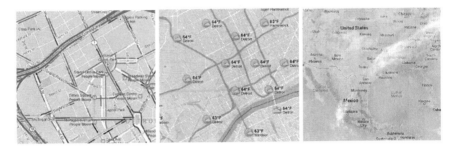

The Traffic Layer

We'll start with traffic, and this one is done in an extremely simple fashion. After initializing our map, you will want to create our new traffic layer object, and in the second line, attach it to the current map.

```
var traffic = new google.maps.TrafficLayer();
traffic.setMap(map);
```

Weather Options

Weather maps are almost identically as simple to create, though it should be noted, you won't see these until you zoom out to a level of 12 or lower. This example sets up the map options first, assigning it to the current map, and then setting the temperature unit to Fahrenheit, instead of the default Celsius.

```
var weatherOptions = {
   map: map,
   temperatureUnits:
google.maps.weather.TemperatureUnit.FAHRENHEIT
}
var weather = new
google.maps.weather.WeatherLayer(weatherOptions);
```

Additionally, clicking on any of the weather points will bring up a five day forecast with highs and lows. However, if you'd like to change this default behavior, you can add a listener for the weather layer when a user clicks a weather icon on the map. From that point, you can retrieve the current weather conditions (day, high, low, humidity, current temperature, wind speed, etc.), the forecast, and the name of the location.

The Cloud Layer

Lastly, the cloud layer. This one looks great for maps that are zoomed out, and just like the weather, won't show up until you zoom out to a level of 6 or lower. In the code below, just like the traffic layer, creates the cloud layer in the first line, then attaches it to the map in the second line.

```
var cloudLayer = new google.maps.weather.CloudLayer();
cloudLayer.setMap(map);
```

In the example provided with this section, start zooming out, and you'll see new items that continue to pop up.

Showing the elevation

Elevations can be useful for a number of reasons. If you're tracking an exercise route a simple point A and point B just don't give you the details you'd like, or if you'd like a simple visualization of the change in elevation over a distance, elevations can create some interesting things. In this example, we'll create a very simple tool to show you such a visualization.

The first step is initializing our elevation service.

```
var elevService = new google.maps.ElevationService()
```

Now for this example, we'll need two points. Selecting two cities that span across Michigan, I chose Detroit and Grand Rapids and found their latitude and longitude using the lookup tool we built in chapter 3. Now that we have the points, we'll create our markers and a polyline to keep things looking nice.

Our next step is to create the elevation points. This is done by extending our variable for the elevation service, calling the "getElevationAlongPath" function. In this function we can pass options for the path, and a number of steps we want to pull, we will also define our callback function that will receive the results (elevations on each step), and the status of the request which notes if the request was successful.

```
elevService.getElevationAlongPath({
    path: [grandrap.getPosition(), detr.getPosition()],
    samples: 30
}, function(res, status){
...
});
```

As you can see above, we get our elevation points in a familiar fashion. Once you have this information, there are a lot of ways you can choose to use it. For this example, I chose a visualization.

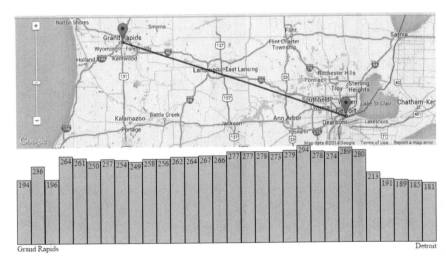

You can view the sample code associated with this segment of the book. I won't go into detail about how it was done since the script isn't specifically about mapping and should be easy enough to understand.

Getting to know the Elevation Service
Error Checking: As noted above, the callback function passes the results as well as a status. You should make sure that the status came back as "OK" before you try to process the results. You can also receive errors noting an invalid request, over the query limit, request denied (likely due to invalid parameters), and unknown errors.

Caps and Limits: Like most of the existing Google features, there is a limit to this service before they want you to start paying. If you are processing points that are frequently recurring it's always best to attempt to cache your results.

Getting the elevation for individual locations
One additional note on the usage worth pointing out. While this example gets the elevation along a point, you can get the elevation of individual points in an almost identical method using the "getElevationForLocations" function. Just like the paths, this function takes an array of points. The only difference is instead of finding the elevation between the points, this will return the elevation for each individual point that is given.

Chapter 10:
Optimizing your code – keeping your maps loading quickly and smoothly

Google has done some incredible things to keep their maps loading as fast as possible, and really invested some heavy resources when you consider the amount of server caching that much go on behind the scenes.

To the same point, all of the functionality does mean you will want to have a level of error checking. A lot of the code that people use just assumes everything goes right, consider what happens when we reach our daily usage caps, or an address doesn't return a longitude or latitude point and errors start becoming visible to your users.

Improving the performance

One of the best ways to improve performance is to reduce the amount of data your map needs to handle, which isn't always easy. Here are some tips to try to keep things clean.

Optimize your data – This is a great place to start. If you consider that at the core of it, your maps are really just reading in and processing a lot of text, then a lot of this becomes much easier. Keep things as short as possible and reuse objects as often as appropriate.

I've built maps with massive amounts of location data for polygons, I found that the precision of my latitude and longitude decimals was greater than necessary, and I was able to improve the performance by changing the precision in my own code to control the length of the position data, sending the shorter numbers of polygon data.

I've run into this as well with info windows to a lesser degree. Everything in the info window mark-up must be passed into the map, so set classes instead of inline styles.

Additionally, if you're using your own marker images, make sure they're sized appropriately. There's no reason to use an image that's 1000 x 100 pixels if you're scaling it down to 24 x 24.

Sprites – If you're using multiple markers or icons for anything else, consider using sprites. This reduces file sizes and reduces load times, something especially positive when creating maps for mobile.

Fusion Tables – I touched on this before, but have a great example. I mapped out a zip code boundary map for all of the zip codes in my state once. This was a massive amount of polygon data. Without any caching, just pulling it straight from the database for every page load, this would take up to two minutes to load. Even more, once I added some caching, it still took close to two minutes to load, showing me the biggest lag time was with the browsers ability to receive, process and display all of the data. Compared to placing this same data into a fusion table, the load time was reduced to seconds. There are trade offs between speed and the ability to customize your output with these two approaches. If your map is too large to load, then it doesn't really matter what kinds of customizations you have, you just need your maps to load.

Additional Code Add-ons - Looking at additional services is always beneficial. If you have a map with thousands of points loaded in the browser, then consider plug-ins that allow clustering. There are a number of 3rd party scripts that will manage your markers, and group them according to your zoom levels, keeping a lot of load off of the map.

Running error free

Now that you've got the fastest loading maps, you want them to become error free. Google puts caps on everything. Always make sure those are accounted for. Additionally, you may be processing data that just isn't always formatted very well or even complete. These are scenarios you have to make sure you've accounted for.

Mapping – Google allows for 25,000 maps a day. This is a comfortable level for mapping, but depending on your traffic levels, it is a very realistic possibility of reaching those limits. You should always be prepared to meet those limits. Make sure you have a backup plan in the event the map doesn't render on your page.

Geocoding - Always make sure you're ready to catch empty results. This is typically due to a poorly formatted or incomplete address. Coincidentally, have a plan to handle results with multiple addresses. This means checking your results. Don't ever just assume Google will always return a single point on the map for you 100% of the time.

Directions – Directions offer a level of mapping that really focuses on the user and what they need. The only problem is, this has a pretty low cap; just 2,500 uses a day. So if you can't retrieve any more directions, make sure you have a backup plan. Default to showing markers for your start and destination points at the very least. If you don't illustrate that your site hit an error, then users won't typically be aware there was one.

Caching - You should always be prepared to reach your daily caps, even if you're not expecting it. Make sure your code is ready for it. If you're writing a map, regardless of the audience, if you are geocoding an address, cache that point. If you're geocoding the address with each and every page request, then it's just a matter of time before you hit your daily cap and Google will stop returning results. Store that point, and use that in your code. It takes just a little more setup work, but in a world where downtime is devastating to a site, this is an ideal route. Additionally, it will keep your map running faster, since this is one less step that needs to be prepared, and one less bit of data that needs to be retrieved.

The same can be said for directions. When you're creating your directions, these are given an unfortunately low cap. If you hit your caps for directions or can't find the points, you need to be prepared to show something else. In most cases, it's probably just best to default to the single marker on the destination (which could take a request to Google to geocode an address, another cap to watch).

Improving the user experience

I'm sure there will always be more that I can put in here, but there are some nice examples that can be widely used. I've already showed you the "reset button" that resets the map to its starting position and zoom in Chapter 5, here are a few others.

Setting the map bounds – By doing this, you can set the map to zoom and center the map on the active markers. If you're loading random markers, markers based on your current location, or any markers that can be loaded dynamically, this will move the map to make sure that they are centered and the map is zoomed in a way that they are all visible. This is extremely useful, and very simple, making sure the user doesn't miss anything on the map.

First, you will need to create the bounds object. This is an object that simply represents a rectangle with geographic coordinates. For every marker you create, add that position to the bounds by using the extend function. Once you finish adding all of your markers, and adding their positions to the bounds, you will call the map to fit to the bounds with the *fitBounds* function, passing it the loaded bounds object.

```
var bounds = new google.maps.LatLngBounds();
//repeat this for each marker
bounds.extend( new
google.maps.LatLng('42.50397746917532', '-
83.4476220056152'));
```

Once you've done this for each marker, this line will center the map on everything.

```
map.fitBounds( bounds );
```

Chapter 11: Mapping for mobile

Mobile web development has been undoubtedly one of the biggest changes to web development and has come with more force than almost anything in my time as a developer. Smart phones and tablets have nearly doubled their market position in the last year, and currently make up 20% of all web traffic, and it's unlikely that those numbers will be decreasing anytime soon. This is why I wanted to give mobile mapping a chapter all its own.

With developing for mobile as its own topic there are a number of things to consider, but I wanted to highlight some of the main areas and offer my best advice.

Load times - Keeping things loading faster is the first place to start. Cell phones don't typically have a hard line connecting them to the internet. As a general rule, keeping the amount of data you need to transfer down to a minimum will always improve performance.

This is where sprites are extremely useful. They take up less space, and are able to be processed faster. If you're unfamiliar with sprites, this is where you take a number of very small images, and merge them into one large image. To load them you typically specify the visible region of the image. Using sprites will reduce load times since you're now using one single file that needs to be downloaded locally instead of writing 10, 20 or more files. It also reduces the file sizes slightly be cutting out redundant data involved with creating a file, which improves the download speeds.

Even if your images aren't sprites, make sure you're keeping icons or any other images sized appropriately. An obvious way to keep things loading quickly is maintaining smaller file sizes anywhere possible. For example, you shouldn't be placing images that are 2000 x 2000 pixel size on a page, then displaying them at 24 x 24 pixels.

If possible, consider using a fusion table. You lose some control over customizations, but the load times will more than make up for that. Your mobile users will be especially happy.

You should never be pulling data from a database directly unless you know the data has changed. Avoid any unnecessary processing time by making sure you have your points cached and ready to go.

Beyond that, keep your code clean, and remove as much unnecessary code and images from a mobile page as you can.

Processing Power – This is always hard to predict. Some people will really invest in their cell phones, some people won't. Everyone has them for different reasons, but you'll get all of them coming to your site and you need to program things accordingly. If your map is really going to be pushing the performance boundaries of a desktop site, then odds are it'll crash right into the boundaries of most cell phones and their browser capabilities.

Fusion tables can really improve this aspect as well since all of the processing is done on the Google servers. If you can't do a fusion table, make sure your data is cached. If you have to process your code, then generate a list of thousands of markers, then render them in the browser, you'll really start to notice the load times in a less capable browser that may have a slower connection to the internet and less memory to process everything.

Clean and smart code plays into this as well. You shouldn't be geocoding addresses unless it is an unavoidable feature of your application. Extra steps means extra processing and extra time passing data back and forth.

User Interface – Google has made some real strides in improvement for mobile users, but keep in mind, mobile users don't have all the buttons that a desktop user has. This becomes very noticeable when you start looking at the various events for listeners. Try to avoid right click actions it's the same for mouse over and mouse out. Some phones attempt to replicate these, but it's never guaranteed which ones will accept these actions and which ones will not.

Screen sizes are not the same as a desktop screen. Studies have found that mobile devices have had increasing screen sizes, but they're still small. Over the last four years, screen sizes have increased less than an inch from 2.4" in 2010, to 3.3" in 2013. This can make the development a real struggle, and it affects everything for the user experience. Don't try to rely on huge html blocks packed with large graphics. Just cut your map down to the core of what you're trying to show, and then show it.

One source that should really help is setting the viewport. Some browsers will try to zoom or resize a website automatically. This can be extremely helpful, unless you've already attempted to design for mobile. Preventing this resize can be done by using the viewport metatag.

```
<meta name="viewport" content="width=device-width,
initial-scale=1.0"/>
```

Browser Capabilities - We've covered geolocating and this is a perfect example. This is a newer feature that came out with HTML 5, but as of this moment, it isn't an HTML standard. This was implemented by Mozilla, and other browsers have followed the lead. The accuracy of this feature is never perfect. The time it takes to retrieve a location isn't always consistent, and both the accuracy and time it takes to generate a location will vary widely based on your location. If you're using an older phone, it may not even be an option.

This, along with other advanced scripting techniques, will require a bit of caution to move forward with, especially considering if this functionally is tied to critical functionality for your site and the users' mobile browser can't run it properly.

Chapter 12: Taking it a step further

At this point, we've covered all the basics, and you should be in a nice position to start having some fun with the mapping API. Now let's start looking at some examples that'll really help you push yourself forward by applying what we've learned.

Measuring the distance and finding the area

Let's start with a common one. You have a number of points on the map, and you want to find the closest to yourself. The first thing we need to do is create a number of markers and then show your own location. For this, let's modify the example from Chapter 2 with our many markers and mash it up with our example of geolocating from Chapter 6. This will give us a map that shows our location as well as a number of predefined locations.

Now we can start to make it into a useful tool. First, we will need to create a markers array. This isn't the only method, but throughout my time with the Google Maps API, giving yourself a way to manage all of your markers has always been among the most useful approach I've taken. Beyond being able to access your markers in a very straight-forward method, if you are creating your markers dynamically, you can quickly get the total number of markers and manage changes to them without much effort.

Initialize the markers array at the beginning of the function.
```
var markers = new Array();
```

After each marker you create (except for your own), add them to the markers array.
```
markers.push(marker1);
```

Now we can loop through our markers, drawing lines, and marking the distance.

```
var len = markers.length;

for(var i = 0; i < len; i += 1){
   //lets create a polyline
   polyOptions = {
      path: [new google.maps.LatLng(baselat, baselng),
new google.maps.LatLng(markers[i].getPosition().lat(),
markers[i].getPosition().lng())],
      map: map,
      geodesic: true,
      strokeOpacity: 0.2
   }
   new google.maps.Polyline(polyOptions);
   var d = haversine(baselat, baselng,
markers[i].getPosition().lat(),
markers[i].getPosition().lng());
   markers[i].title = markers[i].title+" "+ d +" miles
away";
}
```

You should be familiar with a lot of the above code. Inside of our for loop, we create our polyline with the polyline options. Next, call our distance formula that we'll be creating next. Lastly, for ease and simplicity, add the distance to the title of the marker.

For the distance, luckily, Google has a method already of calculating the distance between two points. I want to include Google's method as well as the formula for calculating the distance, for the times that you don't have access to the Google API.

When we're doing this by hand, we're going to rely on something called the Haversine Formula. This isn't a precise formula, since the earth is round, but not perfectly round. For a general distance from point A to point B, this is among the most widely used formulas that takes that curve of the earth into account.

First we need to create a function for radians. This isn't something built into JavaScript, but fortunately it just takes a second.

```
function toRad(x) {
   return x * Math.PI / 180;
}
```

Next, we create our Haversine Formula. I won't dive into the math of this formula, but if you're interested, this can be found across the internet along with trade-offs to this formula vs. other formulas. While none of them are perfect, this one does appear to be among the most accurate in all general distances, and appears to be the most widely accepted as a result.

We call it with our base position that we detected from the browser, and the position of the current marker. Once it finishes the formula, it returns the distance.

```
function haversine(lat1, lon1, lat2, lon2){
   var R = 6378137; // m
   var x1 = lat2-lat1;
   var dLat = toRad(x1);
   var x2 = lon2-lon1;
   var dLon = toRad(x2);
   var a = Math.sin(dLat/2) * Math.sin(dLat/2) +
Math.cos(toRad(lat1)) * Math.cos(toRad(lat2)) *
Math.sin(dLon/2) * Math.sin(dLon/2);
   var c = 2 * Math.atan2(Math.sqrt(a), Math.sqrt(1-a));
   var d = R * c;
   return d;
}
```

If you wanted to take this further, we could make decisions based on how to display the markers based on their distance.

Why the markers array?

This is something I wanted to bring into the chapter, as it's a very useful method of dealing with multiple markers. It's true that we could have performed this calculation as we created each marker, but this allowed you to structure your processes; first the markers, then the math. You may have other applications that will perform other functions. Having a nice way to access all of your markers for any purpose is an extremely useful resource.

Getting the Area

This is another useful feature in the Google Maps API. If you're mapping out state owned property, school districts, or even a state as a whole, this will let you get an approximate area of that area.

This example will take three parts, creating out polygon coordinates, creating our polygon, and lastly, a listener that will calculate and display the area.

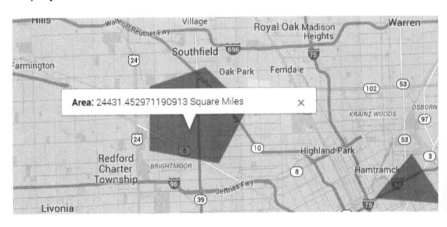

For these coordinates, I just created a random pentagon on the map. The location and the size aren't based on anything.

```
var polyCoords = [new
google.maps.LatLng(42.449808084816, -83.2646942138671),
   new google.maps.LatLng(42.40672766092, -83.26538085),
   new google.maps.LatLng(42.39760094901, -83.20014953),
   new google.maps.LatLng(42.43460661010, -83.17268371),
   new google.maps.LatLng(42.46247316292, -83.212509155)
];
```

Next, we create our polygon just as we've don't in the past.

```
polygon = new google.maps.Polygon({
  paths: polyCoords,
  map: map,
  strokeColor: '#00ff00',
  strokeOpacity: '0.8',
  strokeWeight: '1',
  fillColor: '#0000ff',
  fillOpacity: '0.5'
});
```

Finally we create out listener. When we click on the polygon, this will open an info window at the location of the click. This listener will calculate the area of the polygon and then display it.

When running the calculation, we send the computeArea function our polygon coordinates. It assumes the radius of the earth as meters, so it will return meters squared. After that, it's a quick calculation to convert our answer into miles.

```
listener = google.maps.event.addListener(polygon,
'click', function(event) {
  //get the distance
  var area =
google.maps.geometry.spherical.computeArea(polyCoords);
  //convert this from meters to miles
  area = area * 0.00062137;
  infowindow.setContent("<div
style='width:300px;'><strong>Area: </strong>"+ area +"
Square Miles</div>");
  infowindow.setPosition(event.latLng);
  infowindow.open(map);
});
```

Simulating GPS directions

You're looking at building a directions tool to add to a client's site, something on mobile and there's an option for directions. Instead of just linking to a page on Google's servers, you want to really show something useful. You want to include live directions, as well as active visual tracking while you drive.

Set up the page
Since this will also be used with mobile users, let's make sure to call the viewport, so that we can render as best we can with everyone.

```
<meta name="viewport" content="width=device-width,
initial-scale=1.0"/>
```

We also need to create two containers this time, one for our map, and one for the written directions.

```
<div id="maping" style="width: 100%;">
  <div id="mymap" style="height: 250px;"></div>
  <div id="mymapdirection" style="height:auto;
width:100%; margin-top:5px;"></div>
</div>
```

We'll need to initialize our map with the current browser location of our user, and we should already have the destination, since this is the businesses location.

Getting the starting position

We'll use our browser location function to initialize the map like we've done in the past, passing along the browser coordinates, or in the event that it fails, some default coordinates. This example will time out in five seconds if it can't retrieve a location. Instead of passing the latitude and longitude as separate variables like we've done in the past, it will send a longitude and latitude object.

```
function yourPosition(){
  if(navigator.geolocation) {
navigator.geolocation.getCurrentPosition(function(posit
ion) {
      var position = new
google.maps.LatLng(position.coords.latitude,
position.coords.longitude);
      initialize(position);
    },
    function(position) {
      var position = new
google.maps.LatLng('42.3316033749', '-83.04630989280');
      initialize(position);
    },
    {maximumAge:5000, timeout:5000,
enableHighAccuracy:true});
  }
  else{ //load with a default view of Detroit
    var position = new
google.maps.LatLng('42.3316033749', '-83.04630989280');
    initialize(position);
  }}
```

68

Tracking our user

I'm going to skip the explanation of initializing the map as well as creating the directions as we've covered both of these, but I will make a specific note on something for this chapter. Creating a global variable, "var base", will be a marker based on your current location. Once you've created this marker, you will want to start your tracking.

```
setTimeout(currentPosition,10000);
```

This function is nearly identical to the yourPosition() function, except that it doesn't initialize the map. It sets the position of the base marker, then sets another 10 second time out to call itself.

```
function currentPosition(){
  if(navigator.geolocation) {

navigator.geolocation.getCurrentPosition(function(posit
ion) {
        var position = new
google.maps.LatLng(position.coords.latitude,
position.coords.longitude);
        base.setPosition(position);
        console.log("Current Position:
"+base.getPosition());
        setTimeout(currentPosition,10000);
    },
    function(position) {
      var position = new
google.maps.LatLng('42.3316033', '-83.04630989');
        base.setPosition(position);
        console.log("Current Position:
"+base.getPosition());
        setTimeout(currentPosition,10000);
    },
    {maximumAge:0, timeout:10000,
enableHighAccuracy:true});
  }
  else{
    //load with a default view of Detroit
    pos = new google.maps.LatLng('42.331', '-83.0463');
    base.setPosition(pos);
    console.log("Position: "+base.getPosition());
    setTimeout(currentPosition,10000);
  }
}
```

More Discussion

I chose to use setTimeout instead of a single setInterval call because of how inconsistent the browser location can run. I am giving the function a 10 second time out before starting the next interval. Otherwise this would run the risk of stacking these calls on top of each other, which can cause inconsistent results (in this case, jumpy markers), and lead to memory leaks.

Lastly, if you test this, the location may seem inconsistent at times. This is one thing that should only improve over time since publishing this book. Geolocating is still a very new ability even if it is supported by most browsers. Furthermore, every phone has different levels of accuracy, as well as different methods of finding their current location. Overall, I've been pleasantly satisfied with the results, but everyone should be aware that it's not yet a perfected method.

In the previous code example, you'll also see the current position is being reported in the browser console each time. I chose to do this for developer purposes. If you're sitting at a desktop computer, you'll be able to see the script actively running, even if you don't see the dot moving around with you.

Sorting and organizing your markers

At some point I found myself mapping out tables with a few thousand markers. I needed a way to search for individual markers, with a better method then just looking on the map and hoping to click it. I needed a way to organize and search for the data the markers represented. As a result, I created a way to display a table below the map that was sortable. Taking it a step further, it can also interact fully with the map above. This table was able to extend real-life information for the data the marker was representing while adding some useful functionality.

This one has a number of steps, and I'm going to trim my code down to make it somewhat specific to this example. Start with your markers. For this example, I'm going to map out the 83 counties in Michigan, but just do it with markers. I'll also attach some 2010 census data to them so that we have some info to sort through. Typically I'll do this with a combination of server side scripts to generate my markers, but in this case, I'll spend a little extra time and do it all by hand.

Setting up the Document

We all know how to initialize our map, so I won't bother showing you that, but we do need to include our data and initialize some variables for this one. Most of this is pretty self-explanatory, but just in case, read the descriptions comments below.

```
var markers = new Array(); //container for our markers
var infowindow; //single info window object
var headers = ['County', 'Created', 'Population',
'Area', 'Density']; //labels for our table
//used to keep track of the current sort direction of
our columns
var Sort1 = "desc";
var Sort2 = "asc";
var Sort3 = "asc";
var Sort4 = "asc";
var Sort5 = "asc";
```

Populating the Data

I've attached it in an external JS file. Every county makes a call to an addMarkerFunction with a preset of data. I retrieved the position data by Geocoding, using the same method described in Chapter 3.

```
addMapMarker('Wayne County', '1815', '1820584', '672',
'42.2790746', '-83.33618799999999');
```

The addMapMarker function is created just for this example, but can be crafted to accept more universal examples. This creates our markers, adds a little additional information, which is an incredibly easy task to do since markers are objects, and objects can be assigned new variables in such a simple method. Then we add a listener with the basic information, and push the marker into our markers array.

```
function addMapMarker(county, created, population,
area, lat, lng){
    var marker = new google.maps.Marker({
        position: new google.maps.LatLng(lat, lng),
        map: map,
        title: county
    });

    //define our additional fields
    marker.created = created;
    marker.population = population;
    marker.area = area;
    marker.density = (population/area).toFixed(2);

    listener = google.maps.event.addListener(marker,
'click', function() {
        infowindow.setContent("<div
style='width:300px;'><h2>"+ county +"</h2>Population:
"+population+"<br>Area: "+area+"<br>Established:
"+created+"</div>");
        infowindow.open(map,marker);
    });
    markers.push(marker);
}
```

Printing the Content

Now that we've created our markers and added them to our array, let's build our sortable table. We do this by making a call to our buildSort function. This function creates the actual HTML for our table. We take the data as it was created. In this case, the data was sorted by the County name.

The first loop builds the table headers. These are manually controlled for this example, and are placed with JavaScript calls to the sort function. This is necessary to know which column we're sorting as well as tracking the direction we are currently sorting.

The second loop will place all of the records. Here you can see each of the custom fields being placed. Notice the event trigger, "`<a onclick="google.maps.event.trigger(markers['+ i +'], \'click\')">'+markers[i].title+'</a>`". When clicking on any of the county names, this will trigger a marker click, opening the info window. This is an incredibly useful technique, and can be applied to any event for any object.

Lastly, we grab our table container and place the HTML. This function will be called every time we perform a search, so it's important to realize that the content must be rewritten every time.

```
function buildSort(){
  var content = '';
  //populate the headers
  var len = headers.length;
  content += '<table style="width:100%;">';
  content += '<tr>';
  for(var i = 0; i < len; i += 1){
    content += '<th><a href="JavaScript:sortBy(\''+
(i+1) +'\');">'+headers[i]+'</a></th>';
  }
  content += '</tr>';
  //populate the contents
  var len = markers.length;
  for(var i = 0; i < len; i += 1){
    content += '<tr>';
    content += '<td><a
onclick="google.maps.event.trigger(markers['+ i +'],
\'click\')">'+markers[i].title+'</a></td>';
    content += '<td style="text-
align:right;">'+markers[i].created+'</td>';
    content += '<td style="text-
align:right;">'+markers[i].population+'</td>';
    content += '<td style="text-
align:right;">'+markers[i].area+'</td>';
    content += '<td style="text-
align:right;">'+markers[i].density+'</td>';
    content += '</tr>';
  }
  content += '</table>';
  var container = document.getElementById('tableized');
  container.innerHTML = content;
}
```

So far we've created our map with the markers. We've also printed the table below, and added all of the records.

<u>Now it's time for the sorting!</u>
I didn't want to show the repetitive portions, but I wanted to show you enough to see how this was done. There is a sortBy function that captures everything. This is because this is a fairly repetitive process, with slight differences. This will call our custom sort functions. Since the markers are in an array, we're able to rearrange them with a great deal of ease. Then we look at the sort order to determine what direction we're sorting in, and set the current sort direction for that column respectively. Then, since we just sorted a column, we reset the sorting direction for the other columns. Lastly, with the array in a new order, we reprint the table of data. The user sees it as if we're re-arranging everything, but we're actually rebuilding the entire thing. This is necessary since the marker indexes will no longer line up with the previous table data now that it's been sorted based on different info.

```
function sortBy(field){
  //run the sort function
  if(field == "1"){
    markers.sort(sortBy1);
    if(Sort1 == "desc"){
      markers.reverse();
      Sort1 = "asc";
    }
    else{
      Sort1 = "desc";
    }
    //reset the others
    Sort2 = "asc";
    Sort3 = "asc";
    Sort4 = "asc";
    Sort5 = "asc";
  }
  ......
  //redraw the area
  buildSort();
}
```

The actual sorting function. These can be tedious if you've never done them before, but you're basically checking what comes first. This is a pretty specific test, but this could be written to accept more generic data by assigning data types, testing for those and sorting accordingly. In this example, I built each sort function to sort by the specific field instead of making it universal.

```
function sortBy1(a, b) {
  a = a.title.toLowerCase();
  b = b.title.toLowerCase();
  return a == b ? 0 : (a < b ? -1 : 1);
}
```

More Discussion

It could be argued that this doesn't pertain specifically to mapping since really the only mapping we did was place some markers on a map, and trigger events from external clicks, but I thought this was a worthwhile example since it extended the mapping abilities. This can be extended to a far greater level if you want; enabling true searches, filtering that was reflected on the table as well as the map. Having all of your markers stored in a markers array gives you some really great versatility.

Building a polygon generator

Google does a lot to make things as simple as possible, but why not make them even easier? Polygons are great, but they are tedious to map out. When I want to produce large scale maps, I want to be able to produce them quickly. To really simplify the process, I'd like to have everything done in a visual fashion. Why not build our own tool to generate polygons?

The Plan

Build a tool that lets you visually create a polygon, then give you the embed code. We will want to input coordinates by clicking the map or placing a geocoded marker. In addition to this, we'll want to be able to input an address to geocode into a point for a polygon as well. In the event that we click on the wrong spot, we'll want to be able to drag that polygon coordinate back to the correct position. We won't get too complex, but we'll be able create something extremely useful.

The real power in this one comes from the listeners. Each time you click the map we'll create a new marker. These markers will connect each point on the polygon. We'll allow the user to drag the positions. Once you're happy with your polygon, you will be able to hit a button to spit out polygon data.

Setting up the Document

I won't go into the basics of how to place a map on the page, but I will tell you what we'll need to do next... Initialize your variables. We'll need a marker array, polygon variable, and a polygon coordinate array.

```
var markers = new Array();
var polygon;
var polyCoords = new Array();
```

The Listener

The main listener for this task goes to the map itself. We'll need to create a listener that will create a new marker at the position of mouse click. Once created, we'll give it an index, and add those coordinates to the polyCoords array, and re-assign the path array to our polygon to show the new path. For simplicity, we'll place a lot of this in its own function.

```
listener = google.maps.event.addListener(map, 'click',
function(event) {
  newPolyMarker(event.latLng);
});

function newPolyMarker(latLngPoint){
  var marker = new google.maps.Marker({
    position: latLngPoint,
    map: map,
    title: 'Marker',
    draggable: true
  });
  markers.push(marker);
  //redraw the polygon
  polyCoords.push(latLngPoint);
  polygon.setPath(polyCoords);
}
```

This will let us trace our polygons, but in the event that someone clicks in the wrong spot, we'll want to be able to correct that, so let's add the option to drag our polygons. Inside of the listener code above, we'll need to add another listener for that marker specifically. This will track the index of the marker, and as we move it, update the position of the polygonCoords and send them to the polygon.

```
marker.index = markers.length;
listener2 = google.maps.event.addListener(marker,
'drag', function(event) {
  polyCoords[marker.index] = event.latLng;
  polygon.setPath(polyCoords);
});
```

Adding the Geocoding

For this we can take the code almost hand-in-hand from our previous chapter on geocoding. We'll use the same function that allows us to get the location object from an address, with just a few changes to fit this example.

```
function getAddressLatLng(){
  var geocoder = new google.maps.Geocoder();
  var address =
document.getElementById("markerAddress").value;
  geocoder.geocode( { 'address': address},
function(results, status) {
    if (status == google.maps.GeocoderStatus.OK) {
      var input =
String(results[0].geometry.location);
      newPolyMarker(results[0].geometry.location);
    }
    else {
      alert("Geocode was not successful for the
following reason: " + status);
    }
  });
}
```

Generating the Embed Code

All the hard parts are done; now we just need to generate our embed code to place the polygon into our other maps. For this process, we'll create a function as well. We'll have one button to trigger the function, and a text box to copy/paste the code.

This function is very simple in how it's created. We'll loop through the array of coordinates. Once we've generated the embed code, we'll wrap the rest of the polygon codes around it. As you can see below this doesn't have much error checking. It shouldn't be necessary for this example, if we have an empty array or coordinates, then we'll generate code that reflects that.

```
function getPolyCode(){
  var len = polyCoords.length;
  var i = 0;
  var content = 'var polyCoords = [';
  var polyStr = '';
  for(i = 0; i < len; i += 1){
    polyStr += "new
google.maps.LatLng"+polyCoords[i]+",\n";
  }
  //take off that last comma
  polyStr = polyStr.substring(0,(polyStr.length-2));
  content += polyStr+"];"
  content += "\npolygon=new google.maps.Polygon({\n
paths: polyCoords,\n  map: map,\n })；";
  var polyCode = document.getElementById("polyCode");
  polyCode.value = content;
}
```

Taking it Further
This is a very basic example, but still a huge time saver when you don't have polygon data being provided to you. That being said, there is still a lot that you could do to this.

- Extending polygon options: If you wanted to give the polygons some context to the users who would see them, you could add input fields for additional polygon options. Creating a title, description, or setting display options can all add value to the end user. This can be done in the last step while generating the polygon embed code by creating fields that would be associated with the polygon.

- Undo button: This would be very simple to add, depending on how smart you wanted it to be. If you just wanted to undo placing a new marker/polygon coordinate, then you could have an undo button that on each click, would call an undo function. This function would simply remove the last marker from the markers array, as well as the last polygon coordinate.

- Inserting polygon points anywhere: If you created a poly line between the markers, you could track the clicks and insert a marker based on the position of the click. You would also need each line to hold a reference to the two connected markers, also as if you were creating a visual linked list.

I find that when we start talking about creating wizards, the level of depth you can include can be as limitless as you want. Once you start making them more advanced you can start looking at automation, error checking, and even checks to make sure the proper workflow has been taken when adding information about the area you are mapping out.

Filtering your markers by category

One very useful feature of mapping large amounts of information is being able to filter it. To do this we can take advantage of how we build our maps. Having a thought out structure can be extremely beneficial.

In this example, we'll build a map for the outdoor enthusiast. We'll map out 25 locations at random for kayak rentals, national parks, and nature parks. At the top we'll have options to toggle what is currently visible.

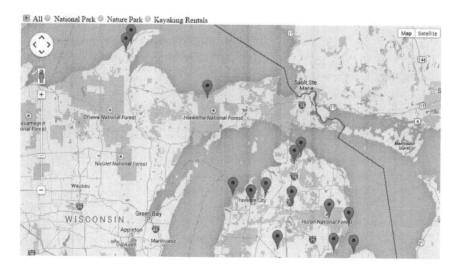

First we need to do the setup. We'll need our map container as well as our initializing function. We'll also want to add all of our markers as a starting point. This can be done simply with a function call to reduce redundant coding.

```
function addMarker(title, address, lat, lng, category){
    var marker = new google.maps.Marker({
        position: new google.maps.LatLng(lat, lng),
        map: map,
        title: title
    });
    marker.category = category;
    markers.push(marker);
}

addMarker('Sleeping Bear Dunes', '6748 Dune Hwy, Glen
Arbor, MI 49636', 44.8825136, -86.0411025, 'National
Park');
addMarker('Keweenaw National Park', 'Calumet Township,
MI 49913', 47.246667, -88.453889, 'National Park');
......
```

The function to add our markers is a very basic function that accepts a title, address, position points, and a category. As you can see above, because a marker is an object, you can define new parameters for it, which is how we add the category property. Before we set the category, this parameter did not exist for that marker. Another important step in this function is adding each marker into an array of markers for easy marker management. This may not seem crucial now, but will be something we rely on for the next couple of steps.

After that, you can see the calls to the function to place them on the map. This method does require a watch for typos with the self-defining categories, but the trade-off is that it will allow you to expand on the categories fairly easily.

This is a good time to remind you of the importance of thoughtful structure. In the beginning of this book, we added our markers individually. Doing that gave a clear picture of how to add a marker. At this point that should be a simple task, so we are cleaning up our code to make it less redundant and easier to scale. Having a function to handle the additions makes our code a lot cleaner. It eliminates redundant code, and allows up to handle changes to the functionality for a lot of places in a single step. The markers index also gives us a way to track every marker. This is incredibly important if we want to loop through these markers for any potential reason… such as changing their visibility!

Now that we've added our markers, we'll also want to have our filter selectors placed at the top of the page. Since we created our markers with an idea of limitless categories, we'll build the selectors from the current categories. This method will automatically create a new filter trigger for any categories you create, instead of requiring you to hand coding each selector individually.

```
function buildFilters(){
    var output = '<label><input type="radio"
name="toggle" onClick="show(\'all\')"> All</label>';
    var filters = []; //initialize our filter container
    //loop through our markers, get the categories
    var len = markers.length;
    var i = 0;
    for(i = 0; i < len; i += 1){
        if(filters.indexOf(markers[i].category) < 0){
            //we have new filter
            output += '<label><input type="radio"
name="toggle"
onClick="show(\''+markers[i].category+'\')">
'+markers[i].category+'</label>';
            //now we add it to the filters array
            filters.push(markers[i].category);
        }
    }
    //now we set the content
    var filterBox = document.getElementById('filters');
    filterBox.innerHTML = output;
}
```

This function loops through our markers array. It has an output string that handles each filter and a filter array to track the filters we've already handled. Each new filter it detects, creates the code for a radio button that has an onClick function to update the visual filters based on the category. It's worth noting that because sometimes we just want it all, this has one pre-defined output, the "All" option. This is hard coded, and will show as the first option when it pushes the output to the user.

Lastly is our filter function. As said, this will be called when users click on the radio buttons. It will receive the category, and change the marker visibility based on that category.

```
function show(what){
  //loop through our markers, display the matches
  var len = markers.length;
  var i = 0;
  for(i = 0; i < len; i += 1){
    if(what == "all"){ //show the markers
      markers[i].setVisible(true);
    }
    else if(markers[i].category == what){ //show this
      markers[i].setVisible(true);
    }
    else{ //hide this marker
      markers[i].setVisible(false);
    }
  }
}
```

This loops through the array in an identical fashion to our filter builder and has the same pre-defined option for the "all" category. If the filter is sent "all", then it loops through the markers, and setting them all to display. Otherwise, it will compare the marker category to the one it was sent, and display it if it's a match or hide it if it isn't.

This simple feature isn't a specific mapping capability, but when you have a map with over 100 or 1000 points on a map, odds are, you'll want a way to be able to filter the data down. This is something that's extremely simple to achieve when you build your code with expandability in mind.

Chapter 13: What is already out there for mapping?

Now that we've got a good idea of some of the more convenient tools, we should take a look at some of the common 3rd party tools out there for Google Maps.

Clustering

Clustering by concept is exactly as it sounds. If you have a map with 1000 markers that are very close to each other, then clustering shows you one large marker to represent many markers Adding text, color, and adjusting the size, you can easily identify how many markers the single cluster might contain.

There are a number of implementations out there, but three of my favorites have been the V2 and V3 of MarkerClusterer by Xiaoxi Wu and Luke Mahe respectively. In this example, we'll use MarkerClustererPlus by Gary Little. This is backwards compatible with the other two plug-ins, and adds some extra functionality.

Clustering not just from a visual perspective, it can help your maps load faster. For example, if you have 10,000 markers packed together on a map, it takes a lot of load off of the browser and the map if you're only rendering a few markers when clustering.

We'll build off an example from Chapter 2 since we have some markers already created. The first thing we'll do is add the plug-in.

```
<script src="markerclusterer.js"
type="text/javascript"></script>
```

Creating the actual clustering object is handled in a similar fashion to creating most objects with the Google Maps API. Define the options, then send them in the initializing call for the object.

Below we set our grid size. If you could imagine the map as a grid, the Clusterer will break down its clusters based on how many markers are in that grid. The maxZoom level specifies when the clusterer will stop being active. After all, as you zoom in, you eventually stop seeing such strong groupings of markers.

In the initializing call, you assign it to the current map, send it the markers array, and the options.

```
var mcOptions = {gridSize: 50, maxZoom: 15};
var mc = new MarkerClusterer(map, markers, mcOptions);
```

Customizing the Clustering

One really nice thing about the Clusterer is how much control it gives you over everything. The two that you will most likely want to redefine are the cluster icons and the cluster number levels.

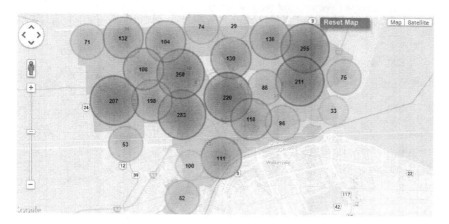

This is a clustering example I had done in the past. This uses custom markers and calculations for the clustering levels.

Custom icons can be sent in an array of JSON objects. The three most basic options are the width, height, and the url to the image, but there are far more options for the image as well as the font style settings.

Below you can see the example, condensed for print. The full code can be seen in the examples. You can see the options to initialize the cluster, but there are also style indexes. You can define as many of these as you want.

```
var mcOptions = {
    gridSize: 60, maxZoom: 14, zoomOnClick: false,
    styles: [{height: 128, url: "iconCluster1.png",
width: 128},
        {...}
    ]
};
```

In addition to defining the styling to customize the cluster markers, you can also redefine the calculator that creates the indexes. This is especially useful for non-uniform ranges or very specific ranges. After initializing the clusterer, set the calculator. This will be a new function that processes everything.

```
mc.setCalculator(Calculator2);
```

We will also need to create the calculator function.

```
var Calculator2 = function (themarkers, numStyles) {
    var index = 0;
    var count = themarkers.length;
    if(count > 0 && count < 9){
        index = 0;
    }
    else if(count > 10 && count < 49){
        index = 1;
    }
    ...
    return {text: count, index: index};
}
```

The Clusterer will let you create a map that has a much lower strain on a user's computer. It also keeps a map looking less congested in a very clear fashion. Even better, it lets a user see how many markers are in a specific location at a glance. While performance is a small benefit of this plugin, the user experience is greatly improved.

Chapter 14: What's next for Mapping?

Probably the best place to look for future developments is to look at what Google Maps provides using their own web interface. Simple things like boundary maps for cities and various regions or floor plans for large established tourist locations would be great features to see added to their API. While these aren't available to the public yet through their API, it's easy to speculate that they could become future releases since the technology is already developed.

Currently, Google's mapping API has a strong focus on efficiency. Maps will work nearly seamlessly between desktop and mobile platforms, but there is still a lot more out there. With ever increasing capabilities for digital platforms, we already have APIs for Android and iOS. It's easy to speculate that we'll start seeing greater advances in geolocating and a stronger focus of mapping around the current user.

Additional services could also start to push further too. Currently weather, traffic, and directions are the primary services, but deeper levels of this would require manual entry. Tracking earthquakes or hurricanes for example all require manual entries. Abilities to track specific and detailed weather events could help show very specific weather trends and formations. Timeline options for map and street views would also offer a great ability to show the development of various areas in a very visual way. In the US, adding census data into mapping utilities could allow for many extended uses, from sales tools to projecting the spread of sicknesses. It's worth keeping an eye on Google to see what they keep pushing out for use with their maps API.

Beyond time tracking of past events, deeper levels of integration would be ideal as well. Google is a leader in the tech industry. They have written APIs for nearly everything, and finding ways to integrate those better to work with one another would add a lot of potential features to a map. With APIs for Fitness, Places, and Contacts, there are a lot of options for extending mapping capabilities. Currently you can do a lot to tie these together on your own, but with future developments from Google, these connections may start to be built more natively and additional APIs may be added to the already impressive list.

Chapter 15: Alternatives to the Google Maps API

The Google Maps API has been able to really prove itself as an industry leader. Frequently adding new features, the maps API has been able to grow and exist all over the web. Like everything out there, it has its downsides, the biggest one being that it'll cost higher trafficked sites and there is like everything else, there is a learning curve. So if you aren't sold on the Google Maps API, we wanted to be fair and let you know, there are alternatives!

Bing Maps: For those familiar with Bing, this is the Microsoft branch of mapping. With many comparable features, Bing Maps allows you to geocode an address, find elevations, map a traffic route, or just view the traffic for an area. Just like Google, Bing Maps does have free basic accounts, and paid accounts, thought they do require you to register for an account to use a key in all of your requests. Source: http://www.microsoft.com/maps/

Polymaps: Aimed at building interactive maps, they take advantage of some more recent web browser features. The maps really take advantage of SVG (Scalable Vector Graphics, which are fast loading, and don't lose quality like rasterized graphics). While SVG might be hard to come by for mapping and spatial data, it allows for interactivity. It is also very fast loading and allows for very fast loading, as well as searchable content. This aims for highly visual and interactive maps that are ideal for showing data, but not all of the map features that Google offers are there, such as geocoding, routes, or weather for example.

(Photo courtesy of Polymaps)
Source: http://polymaps.org/

MapQuest: Among the first mapping services on the web. MapQuest offers a range of comparable services to Google Maps. Just like Google Maps, the MapQuest API also offers geocoding, routes, and traffic. They also offer licensed maps and data as a service that can be bought. MapQuest does appear to have an advantage over Google in lower query caps and dragable routes natively supported.
Source: http://developer.mapquest.com/

Mapbox: A mapping platform that focuses more on building embeddable maps, but does offer APIs for various languages. It also gathers a great deal of its information from OpenStreetMap and allows a great deal of parallel features to Google Maps. It offers a lot

of easy tools to customize the appearances, but because it can be a bit more of a packaged approach, you can lose some of the interactive options. This is a great option if you need maps quick and don't have the time to learn another API. Some larger parties use these maps as well, from Foursquare to Pintrest.
Source: https://www.mapbox.com/developers/

Modest Maps: Built to be a strong base for mapping applications. Modest Maps really focuses on creating maps that look nice and can be extended to go further. The implementation is aimed to be very simple, allowing you to add the "extras" if you want them. All of the interactive options seem to be there and the maps are visually more appealing. They have a clean look, but don't fit the same generic look you're used to seeing.

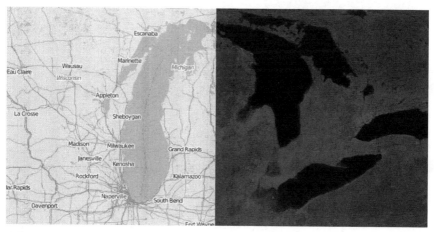

(Photo courtesy of Modest Maps)
Source: http://modestmaps.com/

OpenLayers 3: An API that has been around for a while that can work with other mapping services and gathers a lot of its information from OpenStreetMap, an open project geared towards collecting mapping data. OpenLayers 3 is more advanced, but offers a number of advantages since it can work with multiple APIs. Focused

on vector data, maps typically load very quickly, and have better options to download what is currently visible, something that Google Maps cannot do. The downside to the open environment that gives it so many options is there are a lot of collections of APIs that can be integrated into these maps. This means there's more of a learning curve and more time needed to research what's available.
Source: http://openlayers.org/

Leaflet: is an open-source library based in JavaScript. Designed to allow you to make maps easily, it takes an aim at maps that work on all platforms while working pretty well even with older browsers. This doesn't come as feature packed as Google Maps, but taking the serious aim at getting a light weight map out there regardless of platform is an accomplishment in itself.
Source: http://leafletjs.com/

About the Author

John Sly is a Michigan native and has been working professionally as a web developer in the area for the last 10 years. In that time he has worked on all areas of development and platforms, but found a frequent need for mapping and location based tools. Giving his tools a real world application, he would go on to develop a number of these tools that would receive national recognition. After spending so much time developing large scale systems based largely around the Google Maps API, he decided it was time to prove he could actually write the book on it.

Made in the USA
Middletown, DE
11 August 2015